I0198204

Evelyn Shirley Shuckburgh, Ovid

Selections from Ovid

Evelyn Shirley Shuckburgh, Ovid

Selections from Ovid

ISBN/EAN: 9783337278120

Printed in Europe, USA, Canada, Australia, Japan

Cover: Foto ©Thomas Meinert / pixelio.de

More available books at **www.hansebooks.com**

Elementary Classics.

SELECTIONS FROM

OVID.

Edited for the use of the lower classes in Schools

BY

E. S. SHUCKBURGH, M.A.

LATE FELLOW AND ASSISTANT TUTOR OF EMMANUEL COLLEGE,
CAMBRIDGE; ASSISTANT MASTER AT ETON.

London:
MACMILLAN AND CO.
1879

𝕮ambridge:
PRINTED BY C. J. CLAY, M.A.
AT THE UNIVERSITY PRESS.

INTRODUCTION.

§ 1. *Life of the Poet.*

In the 17th extract of this book is contained most of what we know of the life of Ovid detailed by himself. He was born in the Consulship of Hirtius and Pansa, i.e. B.C. 43, at Sulmo (mod. Sulmona), about 90 miles from Rome, in the country of the Peligni, on the 20th of March. His full name was Publius Ovidius Naso. He always speaks of himself by his cognomen Naso. He tells us that he received from his earliest youth the best and most careful education, and in due time was sent to study rhetoric with the best teachers in Rome; and finally, though he does not mention it in the life of himself, he visited Athens for purposes of study[1]. He had one brother exactly a year older than himself, and their father wished the two boys to study for the profession of Advocates, which was the best way of rising in public life. The family was a well-to-do one, and for many generations the men in it had been included in the Eques-

---

[1] He alludes to this in the description of his voyage to Tomi. Tr. 1, 2, 77, *Non peto quas quondam petii studiosus Athenas.*

trian Order. The elder Ovid, however, died when he was only twenty: and the younger very early showed his distaste for the mode of life which his father planned for him. He tells us, with some pardonable exaggeration, that whenever he tried to compose in prose the words naturally and in spite of himself arranged themselves in metre; that the mysteries of the Muses had an attraction for him which it was impossible to resist; and that his dearest objects of reverence, almost of worship, were the poets of the day. His father tried at first to discourage him from this occupation and to warn him that nothing was to be made of it. But his bent was too strong, and his father's opposition was probably not very determined. And accordingly after serving some minor offices in the states, as one of the *triumviri, decemviri,* and *centumviri,* he declined to try for a curule office which would have given him an entrée into the Senate; and devoted himself wholly to literary pursuits and literary society. His verses soon became the fashion. He appears to have lived in the best Roman society; and from being an enthusiastic neophyte in the set of poets of the day rose to be their leader. Thus he lived at Rome until A.D. 8, when he was 51 years old. In this interval he had been three times married. All we know about this part of his life is that he tells us that his first wife was given him when he was a mere boy, and that they were not happy and were soon divorced. His second wife he also quickly divorced, although he owns that he had nothing to say against her. His third venture was more successful; and with this third wife he appears to have maintained affectionate relations to the day of his death. She did not accompany him into exile, though she wished to do so. But she stayed behind, he infers, for his advantage, probably that she might act as the most trustworthy steward of his property and interests in his absence. Ovid also mentions a daughter, who before his 51st year had been married twice and made him a grandfather twice, having a child by both husbands. Of this daughter we know nothing. Her name has been supposed to be Perilla, from one of Ovid's letters (Trist. 2, 7) addressed to a lady of that name. This however has been with some reason doubted, and it is possible that by *filia* Ovid may mean his third wife's daughter, whom she had by her former husband.

This is what we know of Ovid's life to his 51st year, by which time his father and mother had both died at a very advanced age. In this year in the midst of his prosperity and literary success he was suddenly ordered by a rescript of Augustus to retire to Tomi, on the Black Sea, within a certain day[1]. There was no possibility of refusing to obey such an order; though to a Roman of Ovid's time to quit Rome and to live in such a remote province, was to lose all that made life worth having: and you will see in the extracts from his letters or 'Tristia,' in the third part of this book, what were the particular miseries he felt in this forcible change of residence, and how violent his grief was at being compelled to make it. He lived for nearly ten years from the time he thus left Rome, dying in A.D. 18 at Tomi, from which place he was never allowed to depart. In spite of his lamentable account of himself he appears to

[1] Tomi is the form which has generally been adopted of this word, and it is that used by Suetonius. Ovid however in the only two lines in which he uses it writes *Tomis* (Tr. 3, 9, 33; Ep. e Pont. 4, 14, 59). Two forms also existed in Greek, Τομεύς and Τόμις (Strabo).

have behaved with rather more manliness than we might expect. He to some extent at least carried on his poetical pursuits; he set himself to learn the language of the Tomitae, and even composed some poems in it; and he acquired considerable reputation and esteem among the people, and himself came to feel affection for it, as the retreat of his misfortunes. But to Rome he was never allowed by Augustus, or his successor Tiberius, to return. His punishment was of the milder kind known as *relegatio*, which did not include loss of property or citizenship; but merely a residence in a stated district at a definite distance from Rome. But this latter condition was maintained, in spite of his sometimes abject entreaties, to the day of his death. The ostensible reason for this banishment was the licentiousness of his poem called the ' Ars Amoris ;' and indeed if Augustus chose, as he did at times, to exercise all the functions of a censor, this would be quite reason enough. But Ovid, though he is continually lamenting the harm which this poem had done him, yet always declares that there was another reason. Something he had unwittingly seen or known ; something that was an error and not a crime; something brought home to him by the treason of friends and slaves; something that he will not speak of openly, and which he yet declares to be widely known in Rome ; such is the substance of the hints which he gives as to the secret causes of his punishment. Nothing has been certainly discovered on the subject, but the most probable conjecture is that the offence to Augustus was connected in some way with the misconduct of his grand-daughter Julia, whom he banished in the same year.

§ 2. *Ovid's Writings.*

Up to a few years before his banishment his poems had been all on love subjects.

(1) The AMORES, a series of short elegies chiefly addressed to an imaginary mistress Corinna, which he himself tells us was a fictitious name. These elegies have perhaps been too readily assumed to be founded on personal experiences of the poet.

(2) The EPISTLES, or the HEROINES. Imaginary letters from women, whose misfortunes or intrigues had been famous in the heroic times; and whose stories Ovid found in the various Greek poets and other writers familiar to him.

(3) The ART OF LOVE; the REMEDY FOR LOVE; COSMETICS. It was this group of poems, and especially the first named, that were the ostensible cause of Ovid's punishment. Of this poem it is only necessary to say here that if any poem can deserve such consequences, this one did.

(4) Just before his banishment he had completed the METAMORPHOSES or TRANSFORMATIONS. This is the most elaborate of his works, showing that he had begun to realize that some worthier use might be made of his genius than had yet been the case. It is written in Hexameters, not in Elegiacs, as all his other poems had been, a change which in itself shows that he meant this work to be of a more serious and dignified sort than he had heretofore attempted. At the time of his banishment the METAMORPHOSES were written, but had not received his final revision, and he tells us that in his passionate disgust he burnt his copy, but that friends had already had other copies, and thus preserved the work.

(5) The FASTI, or ROMAN KALENDAR. The Romans kept a careful record, not only of astronomical facts, but of the days marked by political and social events, whether prosperous or disastrous. Augustus was especially interested in this; and it was probably with a primary view of pleasing him that Ovid undertook to make a poetical Kalendar. His plan is to put into verse all the astronomical facts, in accordance with which the almanack is arranged: and to embellish it with an account of the historical transactions commemorated on certain days, whether of a joyful or disastrous character. An example of this is the account of the destruction of the Fabian gens, extract 8. The Fasti were commenced before Ovid's exile, but were not completed till afterwards, and only six months of the twelve were ever accomplished.

(6) The last class of Ovid's writings are the **Poems of his exile.** They consist of (*a*) five books of TRISTIA; short poems, chiefly personal, detailing sometimes the horrors of his voyage, sometimes the disagreeables of his place of exile, sometimes reminiscences of his past life, of the mysterious causes of his punishment, of the friends who were faithful or false to him. (*b*) The IBIS, an elaborate denunciation of some one unnamed who had proved himself an enemy to him in his trouble. In this poem all antiquity is ransacked for instances of dreadful catastrophe to be imprecated on the head of the offender. (*c*) Four books of LETTERS FROM PONTUS, addressed to various friends at Rome, mostly beseeching their friendly intervention with the Emperor to secure the poet's recall.

A few other minor and fragmentary writings were left by Ovid, or have been ascribed to him, of which no particular mention is needed here.

CONTENTS.

OVID.

EARLY ROMAN LEGENDS.

I

[FAST. I. 539—578.]

Evander was said to have migrated to Italy from Arcadia before the Trojan war, and to have built Pallantium on part of the site of Rome. Hercules when driving the cattle of Geryon through Latium is entertained by him. In the night Cacus son of Vulcan, living on the Aventine, steals some of the cattle, and in order to elude Hercules drags them backwards into his cave. Hercules discovers them by the lowing of the stolen oxen, forces his way into the cave and kills Cacus.

PUPPIBUS egressus, Latia stetit exul in herba
    felix, exilium cui locus ille fuit!
nec mora longa fuit, stabant nova tecta; nec alter
    montibus Ausoniis Arcade major erat.
ecce boves illuc Erytheïdas applicat Heros,   5
    emensus longi Claviger orbis iter.

dumque huic hospitium domus est Tegeaea, vagantur
   incustoditae laeta per arva boves.
mane erat; excussus somno Tirynthius hospes
   de numero tauros sentit abesse duos.   10
nulla videt taciti quaerens vestigia furti :
   traxerat aversos Cacus in antra feros;
Cacus Aventinae timor atque infamia silvae,
   non leve finitimis hospitibusque malum.
dira viro facies; vires pro corpore; corpus   15
   grande : pater monstri Mulciber huius erat.
proque domo, longis spelunca recessibus ingens
   abdita, vix ipsis invenienda feris.
ora super postes affixaque brachia pendent,
   squalidaque humanis ossibus albet humus.   20
servata male parte boum Iove natus abibat;
   mugitum rauco furta dedere sono.
'accipio revocamen,' ait; vocemque secutus,
   impia per silvas ultor ad antra venit.
ille aditum fracti praestruxerat obice montis;   25
   vix iuga movissent quinque bis illud opus.
nititur hic humeris, (caelum quoque sederat illis)
   et vastum motu collabefactat onus.
quod simul evulsum est, fragor aethera terruit
         ipsum ;
   ictaque subsedit pondere molis humus.   30
prima movet Cacus collata praelia dextra,
   remque ferox saxis stipitibusque gerit.
quis ubi nil agitur, patrias male fortis ad artes
   confugit, et flammas ore sonante vomit.

quas quoties proflat, spirare Typhoea credas, 35
　et rapidum Aetnaeo fulgur ab igne iaci. .
occupat Alcides ; adductaque clava trinodis
　ter quater adversi sedit in ore viri.
ille cadit, mixtosque vomit cum sanguine fumos;
　et lato moriens pectore plangit humum. 40

II

[FAST. II. 383—420.]

*Numitor and Amulius had been joint kings of Alba Longa.
Amulius deprived the former of his share of the kingly power,
murdered his son, and made his daughter Ilia a Vestal. She
had however twin sons by Mars. The babes Romulus and
Remus are exposed in an ark on the Albula. The waters
subside, and the ark is left high and dry. The babes are
suckled by a wolf.*

Ilia Vestalis caelestia semina partu
　ediderat, patruo regna tenente suo.
is iubet auferri parvos et in amne necari.
　quid facis? ex istis Romulus alter erit.
iussa recusantes peragunt lacrimosa ministri ; 5
　flent tamen, et geminos in loca iussa ferunt.
Albula, quem Tiberim mersus Tiberinus in undis
　reddidit, hibernis forte tumebat aquis.
hic, ubi nunc fora sunt, lintres errare videres ;
　quaque iacent valles, Maxime Circe, tuae. 10
huc ubi venerunt, neque enim procedere possunt
　longius ; ex illis unus, an alter, ait :

'at quam sunt similes! at quam formosus uterque!
  plus tamen ex illis iste vigoris habet.
si genus arguitur vultu, nisi fallit imago,   15
  nescio quem vobis suspicer esse Deum.
at siquis vestrae Deus esset originis auctor,
  in tam praecipiti tempore ferret opem.
ferret opem certe, si non ope mater egeret;
  quae facta est uno mater et orba die.   20
nata simul, peritura simul, simul ite sub undas
  corpora.' desierat, deposuitque sinu.
vagierunt ambo pariter; sentire putares.
  hi redeunt udis in sua tecta genis.
sustinet impositos summa cavus alveus unda: 25
  heu quantum fati parva tabella vehit!
alveus in limo, silvis adpulsus opacis,
  paulatim fluvio deficiente, sedet.
arbor erat, remanent vestigia; quaeque vocatur
  rumina nunc ficus, Romula ficus erat.   30
venit ad expositos mirum! lupa foeta gemellos:
  quis credat pueris non nocuisse feram?
non nocuisse parum est; prodest quoque. quos lupa
        nutrit,
  prodere cognatae sustinuere manus!
constitit, et cauda teneris blanditur alumnis,   35
  et fingit lingua corpora bina sua.
Marte satos scires; timor abfuit: ubera ducunt,
  et sibi permissi lactis aluntur ope.

III

The babes thus saved from drowning grow up as shepherd boys,
and obtain great influence with the neighbouring shepherds.
Having learnt the secret of their birth, they slay their
usurping great-uncle Amulius and restore the kingdom of
Alba to their grandfather Numitor.

Sylvia fit mater : Vestae simulacra feruntur
    virgineas oculis opposuisse manus.
ara deae certe tremuit pariente ministra ;
    et subiit cineres territa flamma suos.
haec ubi cognovit contemptor Amulius aequi,   5
    (nam raptas fratri victor habebat opes)
amne iubet mergi geminos ; scelus unda refugit :
    in sicca pueri destituuntur humo.
lacte quis infantes nescit crevisse ferino,
    et picum expositis saepe tulisse cibos ?   10
non ego te, tantae nutrix Larentia gentis,
    nec taceam vestras, Faustule pauper, opes.
vester honos veniet, cum Larentalia dicam :
    acceptus Geniis illa December habet.
Martia ter senos proles adoleverat annos,   15
    et suberat flavae iam nova barba comae :
omnibus agricolis armentorumque magistris
    Iliadae fratres iura petita dabant.
saepe domum veniunt praedonum sanguine laeti ;
    et redigunt actos in sua rura boves.   20

ut genus audierunt, animos pater editus auget;
   et pudet in paucis nomen habere casis:
Romuleoque cadit trajectus Amulius ense,
   regnaque longaevo restituuntur avo.
moenia conduntur; quae, quamvis parva fuerunt,   25
   non tamen expediit transiluisse Remo.

IV

[FAST. IV. 809—852.]

*The foundation of Rome. Romulus and Remus settle which of
the two is to be the founder of Rome and give it his name, by
an appeal to auspices. The walls are begun. Romulus directs
that anyone leaping over them shall be killed. Remus ignorant
of this leaps over them, and is killed by Celer. His brother
Romulus buries him and mourns for him.* B.C. 753. XI. Kal.
Mai, i.e. 21 *April.*

Iam luerat poenas frater Numitoris, et omne
   pastorum gemino sub duce vulgus erat.
contrahere agrestes, et moenia ponere utrique
   convenit: ambigitur moenia ponat uter.
'nil opus est,' dixit, 'certamine,' Romulus, 'ullo: 5
   magna fides avium est; experiamur aves.'
res placet: alter init nemorosi saxa Palati;
   alter Aventinum mane cacumen adit.
sex Remus, hic volucres bis sex videt ordine: pacto
   statur; et arbitrium Romulus Urbis habet.   10
apta dies legitur, qua moenia signet aratro.
   sacra Palis suberant: inde movetur opus.

fossa fit ad solidum : fruges iaciuntur in ima,
   et de vicino terra petita solo.
fossa repletur humo, plenaeque imponitur ara ;   15
   et novus accenso fungitur igne focus.
inde premens stivam designat moenia sulco ;
   alba iugum niveo cum bove vacca tulit.
vox fuit haec regis : 'condenti Jupiter Urbem,
   et genitor Mavors, Vestaque mater ades !   20
quosque pium est adhibere Deos, advertite cuncti !
   auspicibus vobis hoc mihi surgat opus.
longa sit huic aetas, dominaeque potentia terrae :
   sitque sub hac oriens occiduusque dies.'
ille precabatur : tonitru dedit omina laevo   25
   Jupiter : et laevo fulmina missa polo.
augurio laeti iaciunt fundamina cives ;
   et novus exiguo tempore murus erat.
hoc Celer urget opus ; quem Romulus ipse vocarat,
   'sintque, Celer, curae,' dixerat, 'ista tuae.   30
neve quis aut muros, aut versam vomere terram
   transeat ; audentem talia dede neci.'
quod Remus ignorans, humiles contemnere muros
   coepit ; et, 'His populus,' dicere, 'tutus erit ?'
nec mora, transiluit. rutro Celer occupat ausum :   35
   ille premit duram sanguinolentus humum.
haec ubi rex didicit, lacrimas introrsus obortas
   devorat, et clausum pectore vulnus habet.
flere palam non vult, exemplaque fortia servat :
   'sicque meos muros transeat hostis,' ait.   40

dat tamen exequias : nec iam suspendere fletum
  sustinet ; et pietas dissimulata patet.
osculaque applicuit posito suprema feretro ;
  atque ait : 'invito frater ademte, vale.'

V .

[FAST. II. 721—760.]

*While engaged in the siege of Ardea, the Roman princes are
entertained by Sextus Tarquinius, who suggests the question
as to how their wives are behaving in their absence. Each
speaks in confident praise of his own wife. Collatinus suggests that they shall ride at once to Rome and surprise
them. The wife of Sextus was feasting : Lucretia wife of
Collatinus was weaving among her maidens a cloak for her
husband.*

Cingitur interea Romanis Ardea signis,
  et patitur lentas obsidione moras.
dum vacat, et metuunt hostes committere pugnam,
  luditur in castris ; otia miles agit.
Tarquinius iuvenes socios dapibusque meroque   5
  accipit : atque illis rege creatus ait :
'dum nos difficilis pigro tenet Ardea bello,
  nec sinit ad patrios arma referre Deos ;
ecquid in officio torus est socialis ? et ecquid
  coniugibus nostris mutua cura sumus ? '   10
quisque suam laudat ; studiis certamina crescunt ;
  et fervent multo linguaque corque mero.

surgit, cui clarum dederat Collatia nomen;
  'non opus est verbis; credite rebus!' ait.
'nox superest; tollamur equis, Urbemque petamus.' 15
  dicta placent, frenis impediuntur equi.
pertulerant dominos: regalia protinus illi
  tecta petunt: custos in fore nullus erat.
ecce nurum regis fusis per colla coronis
  inveniunt posito pervigilare mero.   20
inde cito passu petitur Lucretia: nebat;
  ante torum calathi lanaque mollis erant.
lumen ad exiguum famulae data pensa trahebant;
  inter quas tenui sic ait ipsa sono:
'mittenda est domino,—nunc, nunc properate, puellae!   25
  quamprimum nostra facta lacerna manu.
quid tamen auditis? nam plura audire potestis:
  quantum de bello dicitur esse super?
postmodo victa cades: melioribus, Ardea, restas:
  improba, quae nostros cogis abesse viros.   30
sint tantum reduces! sed enim temerarius ille
  est meus, et stricto quolibet ense ruit.
mens abit, et morior, quoties pugnantis imago
  me subit; et gelidum pectora frigus habet.'
desinit in lacrimas, intentaque fila remittit;   35
  in gremio vultum deposuitque suum.
hoc ipsum decuit: lacrimae cecidere pudicae;
  et facies animo dignaque parque fuit.
'pone metum, venio!' coniux ait. illa revixit;
  deque viri collo dulce perpendit onus.   40

VI

[FAST. II. 813—852.]

Lucretia slays herself in consequence of the outrage done her
by Sextus. The Tarquins are driven from Rome: kingly
power abolished: and yearly magistrates substituted. B.C.
509.

Iamque erat orta dies: passis sedet illa capillis,
     ut solet ad nati mater itura rogum.
grandaevumque patrem fido cum coniuge castris
     evocat; et posita venit uterque mora.
utque vident habitum, quae luctus causa requirunt: 5
     cui paret exequias, quove sit icta malo?
illa diu reticet, pudibundaque celat amictu
     ora; fluunt lacrimae more perennis aquae.
hinc pater, hinc coniux lacrimas solantur, et orant,
     indicet: et caeco flentque paventque metu.   10
ter conata loqui, ter destitit; ausaque quarto,
     non oculos ideo sustulit illa suos.
'hoc quoque Tarquinio debebimus? eloquar,' inquit,
     'eloquar infelix dedecus ipsa meum:'
quaeque potest, narrat. restabant ultima: flevit,   15
     et matronales erubuere genae.
dant veniam facto genitor coniuxque coactae.
     'quam,' dixit, 'veniam vos datis, ipsa nego.'
nec mora, celato figit sua pectora ferro;
     et cadit in patrios sanguinolenta pedes.   20
tunc quoque, iam moriens, ne non procumbat honeste,
     respicit; haec etiam cura cadentis erat.

ecce super corpus, communia damna gementes,
  obliti decoris virque paterque iacent.
Brutus adest; tandemque animo sua nomina fallit; 25
  fixaque semianimi corpore tela rapit.
stillantemque tenens generoso sanguine cultrum,
  edidit impavidos ore minante sonos:
'per tibi ego hunc iuro fortem castumque cruorem,
  perque tuos Manes, qui mihi numen erunt; 30
Tarquinium poenas profuga cum stirpe daturum:
  iam satis est virtus dissimulata diu.'
illa iacens ad verba oculos sine lumine movit;
  visaque concussa dicta probare coma.
fertur in exequias animi matrona virilis: 35
  et secum lacrimas, invidiamque trahit.
vulnus inane patet. Brutus clamore Quirites
  concitat, et regis facta nefanda refert.
Tarquinius cum prole fugit. capit annua Consul
  iura: dies regnis illa suprema fuit. 40

VII

[FAST. III. 661—674.]

The plebs to avoid the oppression of the Patricians secede to the
Mons Sacer for the first time (B.C. 494). *Anna supplies them*
with bread.

Haec quoque, quam referam, nostras pervenit ad
    aures
  fama; nec a vera dissidet illa fide.
plebs vetus, et nullis etiam tunc tuta Tribunis,
  fugit; et in Sacri vertice montis abit.

iam quoque, quem secum tulerant, defecerat illos   5
    victus, et humanis usibus apta ceres.
orta suburbanis quaedam fuit Anna Bovillis
    pauper, sed mundae sedulitatis, anus.
illa, levi mitra canos redimita capillos,
    fingebat tremula rustica liba manu.   10
atque ita per populum fumantia mane solebat
    dividere : haec populo copia grata fuit.
pace domi facta signum posuere Perennae,
    quod sibi defectis illa tulisset opem.

VIII

[FAST. II. 195—242.]

*Kaeso Fabius led the Fabii from Rome and established them on
the Cremera. After a year's time they went to Rome on the
Ides of February, and on their way the whole gens, except
one boy, to the number of 306, were slaughtered by an ambuscade of the Veientines near the River Cremera.* B.C. 477.

Haec fuit illa dies, in qua Veientibus arvis
    ter centum Fabii, ter cecidere duo.
una domus vires et onus susceperat Urbis ;
    sumunt gentiles arma professa manus.
egreditur castris miles generosus ab isdem,   5
    e queis dux fieri quilibet aptus erat.
Carmentis portae dextro via proxima Jano est :
    ire per hanc noli, quisquis es ; omen habet.
ut celeri passu Cremeram tetigere rapacem,
    (turbidus hibernis ille fluebat aquis)   10

castra loco pŏnunt: destrictis eusibus ipsi
  Tyrrhenum valido marte per agmen eunt.
non aliter, quam cum Libyca de rupe leones
  invadunt sparsos lata per arva greges.
diffugiunt hostes, inhonestaque vuluera tergo   15
  accipiunt; Tusco sanguine terra rubet.
sic iterum, sic saepe cadunt. ubi vincere aperte
  non datur, insidias armaque caeca parant.
campus erat; campi claudebant ultima colles,
  silvaque montanas occulere apta feras.   20
in medio paucos, armentaque rara relinquunt;
  caetera virgultis abdita turba latet.
ecce, velut torrens undis pluvialibus auctus,
  aut nive, quae zephyro victa repente fluit,
per sata, perque vias fertur; nec, ut ante solebat, 25
  riparum clausas margine finit aquas:
sic Fabii latis vallem discursibus implent:
  quosque vident, spernunt; nec metus alter inest.
quo ruitis, generosa domus? male creditur hosti;
  simplex nobilitas, perfida tela cave.   30
fraude perit virtus; in apertos undique campos
  prosiliunt hostes, et latus omne tenent.
quid faciant pauci contra tot millià fortes?
  quidve, quod in misero tempore restet, habent?
sicut aper silvis longe Laurentibus actus   35
  fulmineo celeres dissipat ore canes;
mox tamen ipse perit: sic non moriuntur inulti;
  vulneraque alterna dantque feruntque manu.

una dies Fabios ad bellum miserat omnes;
    ad bellum missos perdidit una dies.   40
ut tamen Herculeae superessent semina gentis,
    credibile est ipsos consuluisse Deos.
nam puer impubes, et adhuc non utilis armis,
    unus de Fabia gente relictus erat.
scilicet ut posses olim tu, Maxime, nasci;   45
    cui res cunctando restituenda foret.

IX

[FAST. VI. 395—416.]

An altar in the middle of the forum marked the place where the
swamp, called the Lacus Curtius, had once been.

Forte revertebar festis Vestalibus illac,
    qua Nova Romano nunc via iuncta foro est.
huc pede matronam vidi descendere nudo;
    obstupui tacitus, sustinuique gradum.
sensit anus vicina loci; iussumque sedere   5
    alloquitur, quatiens voce tremente caput:
'hoc, ubi nunc fora sunt, udae tenuere paludes;
    amne redundanti fossa madebat aqua.
Curtius ille lacus, siccas qui sustinet aras,
    nunc solida est tellus, sed lacus ante fuit.   10
qua Velabra solent in Circum ducere pompas,
    nil praeter salices cassaque canna fuit.
saepe suburbanas rediens conviva per undas
    cantat, et ad nautas ebria verba iacit.

nondum conveniens diversis iste figuris   15
    nomen ab averso ceperat amne Deus.
hic quoque lucus erat iuncis et arundine densus,
    et pede velato non adeunda palus.
stagna recesserunt, et aquas sua ripa coercet,
    siccaque nunc tellus : mos tamen inde manet.'   20
reddiderat causam. ' valeas, anus optima,' dixi :
    ' quod superest aevi molle sit omne tui.'

X

[Fast. vi. 437—454.]

*The burning of the Temple of Vesta. The Palladium rescued
from the flames by L. Caecilius Metellus, the Pontifex Maximus. B.C. 241.*

Heu quantum timuere Patres, quo tempore Vesta
    arsit, et est adytis obruta paene suis !
flagrabant sancti sceleratis ignibus ignes,
    mistaque erat flammae flamma profana piae.
attonitae flebant, demisso crine, ministrae ;   5
    abstulerat vires corporis ipse timor.
provolat in medium, et magna, ' succurrite,' voce,
    ' non est auxilium flere,' Metellus ait.
' pignora virgineis fatalia tollite palmis :
    non ea sunt voto, sed rapienda manu !   10
me miserum ! dubitatis ?' ait. dubitare videbat ;
    et pavidas posito procubuisse genu.

haurit aquas; tollensque manus, 'ignoscite,' dixit,
  'sacra; vir intrabo non adeunda viro.
si scelus est, in me commissi poena redundet;   15
  sit capitis damno Roma soluta mei.'
dixit, et irrupit : factum Dea rapta probavit ;
  pontificisque sui munere tuta fuit.

THE HEROINES.

XI

[Ep. i. 25—62.]

*Penelope complains that though the Trojan war has been long
over and all the surviving Greek leaders have returned to their
cities, her husband Ulysses cannot be heard of. She describes
the joyful scenes in the several cities when the warriors come
home, and her own terror at hearing of the bold deeds of
Ulysses. But what use, she asks, to her is all this success and
the utter destruction of Troy? She is still a lonely widow,
still searching in vain for Ulysses.*

Argolici rediere duces : altaria fumant :
   ponitur ad patrios barbara praeda deos.
grata ferunt nymphae pro salvis dona maritis : .
   illi victa suis Troica fata canunt.
mirantur iustique senes trepidaeque puellae :   5
   narrantis coniunx pendet ab ore viri.
atque aliquis posita monstrat fera praelia mensa,
   pingit et exiguo Pergama tota mero :

'hac ibat Simois, hac est Sigeïa tellus,
  hic steterat Priami regia celsa senis :   10
illic Aeacides, illic tendebat Ulixes :
  hic lacer admissos terruit Hector equos.'
omnia namque tuo senior te quaerere misso
  retulerat gnato Nestor, at ille mihi.
retulit et ferro Rhesumque Dolonaque caesos,   15
  utque sit hic somno proditus, ille dolo.
ausus es, o nimium nimiumque oblite tuorum,
  Thracia nocturno tangere castra dolo,
totque simul mactare viros, adiutus ab uno !
  at bene cautus eras et memor ante mei ?   20
usque metu micuere sinus, dum victor amicum
  dictus es Ismariis isse per agmen equis.
sed mihi quid prodest vestris disiecta lacertis
  Ilios, et murus quod fuit esse solum,
si maneo qualis Troia durante manebam,   25
  virque mihi dempto fine carendus abest ?
diruta sunt aliis, uni mihi Pergama restant,
  incola captivo quae bove victor arat.
iam seges est, ubi Troia fuit, resecandaque falce
  luxuriat Phrygio sanguine pinguis humus :   30
semisepulta virum curvis feriuntur aratris
  ossa : ruinosas occulit herba domos.
victor abes ; nec scire mihi, quae causa morandi,
  aut in quo lateas ferreus orbe, licet.
quisquis ad haec vertit peregrinam littora puppim, 35
  ille mihi de te multa rogatus abit :
quamque tibi reddat, si te modo viderit usquam,
  traditur huic digitis charta notata meis.

XII

[EP. III. 67—98.]

Briseis has been taken away from Achilles by Agamemnon. Achilles in anger refrains from fighting, and threatens to leave the camp round Troy and go home. Briseis is eager to be reclaimed by him; and says that she is willing to go home with him even as a slave. But what she would best like is that he should accept her restoration which Agamemnon offers and once more fight against the Trojans. She hopes that he will be swayed by her prayers though he has rejected all others, just as Meleager was by those of his wife.

Si tibi iam reditusque placent patriique penates,
  non ego sum classi sarcina magna tuae.
victorem captiva sequar, non nupta maritum :
  est mihi, quae lanas molliat, apta manus.
inter Achaeïadas longe pulcherrima matres			5
  in thalamos coniunx ibit eatque tuos,
digna nurus socero, Iovis Aeginaeque nepote,
  cuique senex Nereus prosocer esse velit.
nos humiles famulaeque tuae data pensa trahemus,
  et minuent plenas stamina nostra colos.			10
exagitet ne me tantum tua, deprecor, uxor,
  quae mihi nescio quo non erit aequa modo;
neve meos coram scindi patiare capillos,
  et leviter dicas 'haec quoque nostra fuit.'
vel patiare licet, dum ne contempta relinquar :		15
  hic mihi vae miserae concutit ossa metus.

quid tamen expectas ? Agamemnona paenitet irae,
   et iacet ante tuos Graecia maesta pedes.
vince animos iramque tuam, qui cetera vincis.
   quid lacerat Danaas impiger Hector opes ?   20
arma cape, Aeacide, sed me tamen ante recepta,
   et preme turbatos Marte favente viros.
propter me mota est, propter me desinat ira:
   simque ego tristitiae causa modusque tuae.
nec tibi turpe puta precibus succumbere nostris. 25
   coniugis Oenides versus in arma prece est.
res audita mihi, nota est tibi : fratribus orba
   devovit nati spemque caputque parens.
bellum erat. ille ferox positis secessit ab armis,
   et patriae rigida mente negavit opem.   30
sola virum coniunx flexit : felicior illa!
   at mea pro nullo pondere verba cadunt.

XIII

[EP. v. 9—36.]

*Oenone, once loved but now deserted by Paris, reminds him of
their former happy companionship, when he was a shepherd on
mount Ida and she though a nymph did not disdain his love.
Then it was she who helped him in the hunt; then he swore to
her eternal fidelity and cut the words of his vow on a poplar
tree.*

Nondum tantus eras, cum te contenta marito
   edita de magno flumine nympha fui.   ˙
qui nunc Priamides,... absit reverentia vero...
   servus eras. servo nubere nympha tuli.

quis tibi monstrabat saltus venatibus aptos,   5
  et tegeret catulos qua fera rupe suos?
retia saepe comes maculis distincta tetendi:
  saepe citos egi per iuga longa canes.
incisae servant a te mea nomina fagi,
  et legor Oenone falce notata tua :   10
et quantum trunci, tantum mea nomina crescunt :
  crescite, et in titulos surgite recta meos.
popule, vive, precor, quae consita margine ripae
  hoc in rugoso cortice carmen habes
'cum. Paris Oenone poterit spirare relicta,   15
  ad fontem Xanthi versa recurret aqua.'
Xanthe, retro propera, versaeque recurrite lymphae!
  sustinet Oenonen deseruisse Paris.
illa dies fatum miserae mihi dixit, ab illa
  pessima mutati coepit amoris hiemps,   20
qua Venus et Iuno, sumptisque decentior armis
  venit in arbitrium nuda Minerva tuum.

XIV

[Ep. vi. 81—98.]

*Hypsipyle, of Lemnos, once beloved by Jason, has heard that he
has deserted her and married Medea, the enchantress. She
was always afraid, she says, of being supplanted by some
Greek woman, but did not expect to be ousted by a foreigner
and a witch. She describes Medea's enchantments.*

Argolidas timui : nocuit -mihi barbara pelex.
  non expectata vulnus ab hoste tuli.

nec facic meritisque placet, sed carmina novit :
  diraque cantata pabula falce metit.
illa reluctantem cursu deducere Lunam   5
  nititur, et tenebris abdere Solis equos.
illa refrenat aquas, obliquaque flumina sistit :
  illa loco silvas vivaque saxa movet.
per tumulos errat passis discincta capillis,
  certaque de tepidis colligit ossa rogis.   10
devovet absentis, simulacraque cerea fingit,
  et miserum tenuis in iecur urget acus,
et quae nescierim melius. male quaeritur herbis
  moribus et forma conciliandus amor.
hanc potes amplecti, thalamoque relictus in uno 15
  impavidus somno nocte silente frui ?
scilicet ut tauros, ita te iuga ferre coegit :
  quaque feros anguis, te quoque mulcet ope.

XV

[Ep. x. 7—44.]

*Ariadne saved Theseus in his contest with the Minotaur, by
  giving him a clue to guide him through the labyrinth. He
  took her with him from Crete, but deserted her on Naxos,
  sailing away while she was asleep. She describes her waking
  and finding him gone, her terror, and her despair.*

Tempus erat, vitrea quo primum terra pruina
  spargitur et tectae fronde queruntur aves :
incertum vigilans, a somno languida, movi
  Thesea prensuras semisupina manus :

nullus erat: referoque manus, iterumque retempto, 5
    perque torum moveo bracchia, nullus erat.
excussere metus somnum: conterrita surgo,
    membraque sunt viduo praecipitata toro.
protinus adductis sonuerunt pectora palmis,
    utque erat e somno turbida, rapta coma est. 10
luna fuit. specto, siquid nisi litora cernam.
    quod videant oculi, nil nisi litus habent.
nunc huc, nunc illuc, et utroque sine ordine
    curro.
    alta puellares tardat arena pedes.
interea toto clamanti litore 'Theseu!' 15
    reddebant nomen concava saxa tuum,
et quotiens ego te, totiens locus ipse vocabat.
    ipse locus miserae ferre volebat opem.
mons fuit: apparent frutices in vertice rari:
    hinc scopulus raucis pendet adesus aquis: 20
ascendo: vires animus dabat: atque ita late
    aequora prospectu metior alta meo.
inde ego... nam ventis quoque sum crudelibus usa...
    vidi praecipiti carbasa tenta noto.
aut vidi, aut certe cum me vidisse putarem, 25
    frigidior glacie semianimisque fui.
nec languere diu patitur dolor: excitor illo,
    excitor et summa Thesea voce voco.
'quo fugis?' exclamo 'scelerate revertere Theseu,
    flecte ratem! numerum non habet illa suum.' 30
haec ego. quod voci deerat, plangore replebam:
    verbera cum verbis mixta fuere meis.

si non audires, ut saltem cernere posses,
  iactatae late signa dedcre manus.
candidaque inposui longae velamina virgae,   35
  scilicet oblitos admonitura mei.
iamque oculis ereptus eras : tum denique flevi.
  torpuerant molles ante dolore genae.

XVI

[EP. XIII. 93—134.]

*There was an oracle that the man of the Greek host who first
touched the soil of Troy should be slain.   Laodamia has
heard of this and writes to her husband Protesilaus warning
him of it and begging him to beware of landing first.   She
tells him that she thinks of him day and night : but that her
dreams of him are terrifying, and she cannot help being
alarmed.   Her foreboding was justified, for Protesilaus was the
first to land and was slain.*

Sors quoque nescio quem fato designat iniquo,
  qui primus Danaum Troada tangat humum.
infelix, quae prima virum lugebit ademptum !
  di faciant, ne tu strenuus esse velis !
inter mille rates tua sit millensima puppis,   5
  iamque fatigatas ultima verset aquas.
hoc quoque praemoneo : de nave novissimus exi :
  non est, quo properas, terra paterna tibi.
cum venies, remoque move veloque carinam,
  inque tuo celerem litore siste gradum !   10

sive latet Phoebus, seu terris altior exstat,
  tu mihi luce dolor, tu mihi nocte venis.
excutior somno, simulacraque noctis adoro :
  nulla caret fumo Thessalis ara meo :
tura damus, lacrimamque super, qua sparsa relucet,   15
  ut solet adfuso surgere flamma mero.
sed cum Troia subit, subeunt ventique fretumque,
  spes bona sollicito victa timore cadit.
hoc quoque, quod venti prohibent exire carinas,
  me movet : invitis ire paratis aquis.   20
quis velit in patriam vento prohibente reverti ?
  a patria pelago vela vetante datis !
ipse suam non praebet iter Neptunus ad urbem.
  quo ruitis ? vestras quisque redite domos !
quo ruitis, Danai ? ventos audite vetantis !   25
  non subiti casus, numinis ista mora est.
quid petitur tanto nisi turpis adultera bello ?
  dum licet, Inachiae vertite vela rates !

OVID'S PERSONAL HISTORY.

XVII

[TR. IV. 10. 1—98.]

Scarcely any ancient poet has taken so much trouble to make himself known to posterity as Ovid has done. In this piece he tells all the facts of his life, and many of his views and feelings. How his father meant him to be a lawyer and politician, but how he was irresistibly drawn to poetry. His literary enthusiasms and associations; his three marriages; the birth of his daughter; the early death of his brother; and finally the blow which fell upon himself—Augustus suddenly and without warning ordering him to go into banishment at Tomi, on the Black Sea, two hundred miles north of Constantinople.

Ille ego, qui fuerim, tenerorum lusor amorum,
    quem legis, ut noris, accipe, Posteritas.
Sulmo mihi patria est, gelidis uberrimus undis,
    millia qui novies distat ab Urbe decem.

editus hic ego sum : necnon, ut tempora noris ;   5
  cum cecidit fato Consul uterque pari.
si quid id est, usque a proavis vetus ordinis heres ;
  non modo Fortunae munere factus eques.
nec stirps prima fui ; (genito iam fratre creatus)
  qui tribus ante quater mensibus ortus erat.   10
lucifer amborum natalibus adfuit idem :
  una celebrata est per duo liba dies.
haec est armiferae festis de quinque Minervae,
  quae fieri pugna prima cruenta solet.
protinus excolimur teneri, curaque parentis   15
  imus ad insignes Urbis ab arte viros.
frater ad eloquium viridi tendebat ab aevo,
  fortia verbosi natus ad arma Fori.
at mihi iam puero coelestia sacra placebant ;
  inque suum furtim Musa trahebat opus.   20
saepe pater dixit, 'studium quid inutile tentas ?
  Maeonides nullas ipse reliquit opes.'
motus eram dictis : totoque Helicone relicto,
  scribere conabar verba soluta modis.
sponte sua numeros carmen veniebat ad aptos :   25
  et, quod tentabam dicere, versus erat.
interea, tacito passu labentibus annis,
  liberior fratri sumta, mihique, toga est :
induiturque humeros cum lato purpura clavo :
  et studium nobis, quod fuit ante, manet.   30
iamque decem vitae frater geminaverat annos,
  cum perit ; et coepi parte carere mei.

cepimus et tenerae primos aetatis honores;
  eque viris quondam pars tribus una fui.
curia restabat: clavi mensura coacta est: 35
  maius erat nostris viribus illud onus.
nec patiens corpus, nec mens fuit apta labori,
  sollicitaeque fugax ambitionis eram:
et petere Aoniae suadebant tuta Sorores
  otia, iudicio semper amata meo.   40
temporis illius colui fovique poetas;
  quotque aderant vates, rebar adesse Deos.
saepe suas volucres legit mihi grandior aevo,
  quaeque necet serpens, quae iuvet herba, Macer.
saepe suos solitus recitare Propertius ignes;   45
  iure sodalitio qui mihi iunctus erat.
Ponticus Heroo, Bassus quoque clarus Iambo,
  dulcia convictus membra fuere mei.
et tenuit nostras numerosus Horatius aures;
  dum ferit Ausonia carmina culta lyra.   50
Vergilium vidi tantum: nec amara Tibullo
  tempus amicitiae fata dedere meae.
successor fuit hic tibi, Galle; Propertius illi.
  quartus ab his serie temporis ipse fui.
utque ego maiores, sic me coluere minores: 55
  notaque non tarde facta Thalia mea est. ⚔.
carmina cum primum populo iuvenilia legi;
  barba resecta mihi bisve semelve fuit.
moverat ingenium, totam cantata per Urbem,
  nomine non vero dicta Corinna mihi.   60

multa quidem scripsi: sed quae vitiosa putavi,
emendaturis ignibus ipse dedi.
tum quoque, cum fugerem, quaedam placitura cremavi,
iratus studio carminibusque meis.
molle, Cupidineis nec inexpugnabile telis 65
cor mihi, quodque levis caussa moveret, erat.
cum tamen hoc essem, minimoque accenderer igni;
nomine sub nostro fabula nulla fuit.
pene mihi puero nec digna, nec utilis, uxor
est data: quae tempus perbreve nupta fuit. 70
illi successit, quamvis sine crimine, coniux;
non tamen in nostro firma futura toro.
ultima, quae mecum seros permansit in annos,
sustinuit coniux exsulis esse viri.
filia me mea bis prima fecunda iuventa, 75
sed non ex uno coniuge, fecit avum.
et iam complerat genitor sua fata; novemque
addiderat lustris altera lustra novem.
non aliter flevi, quam me fleturus ademtum
ille fuit. matri proxima iusta tuli. 80
felices ambo, tempestiveque sepulti,
ante diem poenae quod periere meae!
me quoque felicem, quod non viventibus illis
sum miser; et de me quod doluere nihil!
si tamen exstinctis aliquid, nisi nomina, restat, 85
et gracilis structos effugit umbra rogos;
fama, parentales, si vos mea contigit, umbrae;
et sunt in Stygio crimina nostra foro;

scite, precor, caussam (nec vos mihi fallere fas est)
    errorem iussae, non scelus, esse fugae.   90
manibus id satis est. ad vos studiosa revertor
    pectora, qui vitae quaeritis acta meae.
iam mihi canities, pulsis melioribus annis,
    venerat; antiquas miscueratque comas :
postque meos ortus Pisaea vinctus oliva   95
    abstulerat decies praemia victor equus ;
cum maris Euxini positos ad laeva Tomitas
    quaerere me laesi Principis ira iubet.

XVIII

[TR. I. 3.]

Ovid's last night in Rome. He had been ordered to leave Rome
within a certain day, and the last night has come. He must
go before daybreak. He tears himself away with sorrow and
tears from his wife and friends. His wife wished to go with
him, but this he would not allow.

Cum subit illius tristissima noctis imago,
    quae mihi supremum tempus in Urbe fuit ;
cum repeto noctem, qua tot mihi cara reliqui ;
    labitur ex oculis nunc quoque gutta meis.
iam prope lux aderat, qua me discedere Caesar   5
    finibus extremae iusserat Ausoniae.
nec mens, nec spatium fuerant satis apta paranti :
    torpuerant longa pectora nostra mora.

non mihi servorum, comitis non cura legendi,
   non aptae profugo vestis opisve fuit.   10
non aliter stupui, quam qui Iovis ignibus ictus
   vivit, et est vitae nescius ipse suae.
ut tamen hanc animo nubem dolor ipse removit,
   et tandem sensus convaluere mei;
adloquor extremum moestos abiturus amicos,   15
   qui modo de multis unus et alter erant.
uxor amans flentem flens acrius ipsa tenebat;
   imbre per indignas usque cadente genas.
nata procul Libycis aberat diversa sub oris:
   nec poterat fati certior esse mei.   20
quocumque adspiceres, luctus gemitusque sonabant:
   formaque non taciti funeris intus erat.
femina, virque, meo pueri quoque funere moerent:
   inque domo lacrimas angulus omnis habet.
si licet exemplis in parvo grandibus uti;   25
   haec facies Troiae, cum caperetur, erat.
tum vero coniux, humeris abeuntis inhaerens,
   miscuit haec lacrimis tristia dicta suis:
'non potes avelli: simul ah, simul ibimus,' inquit:
   'te sequar: et coniux exsulis exsul ero.   30
et mihi facta via est: et me capit ultima tellus.
   accedam profugae sarcina parva rati.
te iubet e patria discedere Caesaris ira;
   me pietas. pietas haec mihi Caesar erit.'
talia tentabat: sic et tentaverat ante: 35
   vixque dedit victas utilitate manus.

egredior_ (sive illud erat sine funere ferri)
   squalidus immissis hirta per ora comis.
illa dolore gravis, tenebris narratur obortis
   semianimis media procubuisse domo.   40
utque resurrexit, foedatis pulvere turpi
   crinibus, et gelida membra levavit humo;
se modo, desertos modo complorasse Penates;
   nomen et erepti saepe vocasse viri:
nec gemuisse minus, quam si nataeve meumve   45
   vidisset structos corpus habere rogos:
et voluisse mori, et moriendo ponere sensus:
   respectuque tamen non posuisse mei.
vivat: et absentem, quoniam sic fata tulerunt,
   vivat, et auxilio sublevet usque suo.   50

XIX

[Tr. I. 2. 19—56.]

*A storm at sea which Ovid met with on his voyage towards his
place of exile.*

Me miserum, quanti montes volvuntur aquarum!
   iam iam tacturos sidera summa putes.
quantae diducto subsidunt aequore valles!
   iam iam tacturas Tartara nigra putes.
quocumque adspicias, nihil est nisi pontus et aer,   5
   fluctibus hic tumidus, nubibus ille minax.

inter utrumque fremunt immani turbine venti.
 nescit, cui domino pareat, unda maris.
nam modo purpureo vires capit Eurus ab ortu :
 nunc Zephyrus sero vespere missus adest:　　　10
nunc gelidus sicca Boreas bacchatur ab Arcto :
 nunc Notus adversa proelia fronte gerit.
rector in incerto est : nec, quid fugiatve petatve,
 invenit. ambiguis ars stupet ipsa malis.
scilicet occidimus, nec spes, nisi vana, salutis :　　15
 dumque loquor vultus obruit unda meos.
opprimet hanc animam fluctus : frustraque precanti
 .ore necaturas accipiemus aquas.
at pia nil aliud quam me dolet exsule coniux :
 hoc unum nostri scitque gemitque mali.　　　20
nescit in immenso iactari corpora ponto :
 nescit agi ventis : nescit adesse necem.
o bene, quod non sum mecum conscendere passus :
 ne mihi mors misero bis patienda foret !
at nunc, ut peream, quoniam caret illa periclo,　　25
 dimidia certe parte superstes ero.
hei mihi, quam celeri micuerunt nubila flamma !
 quantus ab aetherio personat axe fragor !
nec levius laterum tabulae feriuntur ab undis,
 quam grave balistae moenia pulsat onus.　　　30
qui venit hic fluctus, fluctus supereminet omnes :
 posterior nono est, undecimoque prior.
nec letum timeo : genus est miserabile leti :
 demite naufragium ; mors mihi munus erit.

est aliquid, fatove suo ferrove cadentem 35
 in solida moriens ponere corpus humo :
et mandare suis, aliqua aut sperare sepulcra,
 et non aequoreis piscibus esse cibum.

XX

[Tr. iii. 3. 1—24.]

*At Tomi Ovid falls ill. The climate does not suit him. There
is no doctor, no proper house nor food, and he is alone and
miserable.*

Haec mea, si casu miraris, epistola quare
 alterius digitis scripta sit : aeger eram.
aeger in extremis ignoti partibus orbis ;
 incertusque meae pene salutis eram.
quid mihi nunc animi dira regione iacenti 5
 inter Sauromatas esse Getasque putes ?
nec coelum patimur, nec aquis adsuevimus istis ;
 terraque nescio quo non placet ipsa modo.
non domus apta satis : non hic cibus utilis aegro :
 nullus, Apollinea qui levet arte malum. 10
non qui soletur, non qui labentia tarde
 tempora narrando fallat, amicus adest.
lassus in extremis iaceo populisque locisque :
 et subit adfecto nunc mihi, quidquid abest.
omnia cum subeant ; vincis tamen omnia, coniux : 15
 et plus in nostro pectore parte tenes.

tc loquor absentem : vox te mea nominat unam :
  nulla venit sine te nox mihi, nulla dies.
quin etiam sic me dicunt aliena locutum,
  ut foret amenti nomen in ore tuum.   20
si iam deficiat suppresso lingua palato,
  vix instillato restituenda mero ;
nuntiet huc aliquis dominam venisse ; resurgam:
  spesque tui nobis caussa vigoris erit.

XXI

[TR. III. 10. 13—66.]

*Further miseries of Tomi. The winter is most severe, and no
sooner is the Ister frozen over than the barbarians who live on
the other side of it pour over and harry the country, carry off
all the miserable belongings of the country people, kill the
inhabitants, and burn their cottages.*

Nix iacet : et iactam nec Sol pluviaeve resolvunt :
  indurat Boreas, perpetuamque facit.
ergo, ubi delicuit nondum prior, altera venit :
  et solet in multis bima manere locis.
tantaque commoti vis est Aquilonis, ut altas   5
  aequet humo turres, tectaque rapta ferat.
pellibus et sutis arcent male frigora braccis ;
  oraque de toto corpore sola patent.
saepe sonant moti glacie pendente capilli,
  et nitet inducto candida barba gelu :   - 10

nudaque consistunt, formam servantia testae,
    vina : nec hausta meri, sed data frusta bibunt.
quid loquar, ut vincti concrescant frigore rivi,
    deque lacu fragiles effodiantur aquae ?   •
ipse, papyrifero qui non angustior amne,   15
    miscetur vasto multa per ora freto,
caeruleos ventis latices durantibus, Hister
    congelat, et tectis in mare serpit aquis.
quaque rates ierant, pedibus nunc itur : et undas
    frigore concretas ungula pulsat equi.   .   20
perque novos pontes subter labentibus undis
    ducunt Sarmatici barbara plaustra boves.
vix equidem credar : sed cum sint praemia falsi
    nulla, ratam testis debet habere fidem.
vidimus ingentem glacie consistere pontum,   25
    lubricaque immotas testa premebat aquas.
nec vidisse sat est.   durum calcavimus aequor :
    undaque non udo sub pede summa fuit.
si tibi tale fretum quondam, Leandre, fuisset ;
    non foret angustae mors tua crimen aquae.   30
tum neque se pandi possunt delphines in auras
    tollere : conantes dura coercet hiemps.
et quamquam Boreas iactatis insonet alis,
    fluctus in obsesso gurgite nullus erit.
inclusaeque gelu stabunt, ut marmore, puppes :   35
    nec poterit rigidas findere remus aquas.
vidimus in glacie pisces haerere ligatos :
    et .pars ex illis tum quoque viva fuit.

sive igitur nimii Boreae vis saeva marinas,
　sive redundatas flumine cogit aquas;　　　　40
protinus, aequato siccis Aquilonibus Histro,
　invehitur celeri barbarus hostis equo :
hostis equo pollens, longeque volante sagitta,
　vicinam late depopulatur humum.
diffugiunt alii; nullisque tuentibus agros,　　45
　incustoditae diripiuntur opes.
ruris opes parvae, pecus, et stridentia plaustra ;
　et quas divitias incola pauper habet.
pars agitur vinctis post tergum capta lacertis,
　respiciens frustra rura Laremque suum.　　50
pars cadit hamatis misere confixa sagittis :
　nam volucri ferro tinctile virus inest.
quae nequeunt secum ferre aut abducere, perdunt :
　et cremat insontes hostica flamma casas.

XXII

[TR. IV. 10. 111—132.]

*In this place, however, he found employment and consolation in
his old pursuit of Poetry. 'Over this,' he says elsewhere,
'Caesar has no jurisdiction.'*

Hic ego, finitimis quamvis circumsoner armis,
　tristia, quo possum, carmine fata levo.
quod, quamvis nemo est, cuius referatur ad aures ;
　sic tamen absumo decipioque diem.

ergo, quod vivo, durisque laboribus obsto,   5
    nec me sollicitae taedia lucis habent,
gratia, Musa, tibi. nam tu solatia praebes;
    tu curae requies, tu medicina mali:
tu dux, tu comes es: tu nos abducis ab Histro;
    in medioque mihi das Helicone locum.   10
tu mihi (quod rarum) vivo sublime dedisti
    nomen; ab exsequiis quod dare Fama solet.
nec, qui detrectat praesentia, Livor iniquo
    ullum de nostris dente momordit opus.
nam, tulerint magnos cum secula nostra poetas, 15
    non fuit ingenio Fama maligna meo.
cumque ego praeponam multos mihi; non minor illis
    dicor: et in toto plurimus orbe legor.
si quid habent igitur vatum praesagia veri;
    protinus ut moriar, non ero, terra, tuus.   20
sive favore tuli, sive hanc ego carmine famam,
    iure tibi grates, candide lector, ago.

EARLY ROMAN LEGENDS.

I

1. **exul]** Evander, of Arcadia, who some years before the Trojan war was said to have come from Pallantium in Arcadia to Latium, and there to have founded a city Pallantium, which afterwards became part of Rome and gave its name to the Palatine.

2. 'How happy was he to have that country (Latium) for his place of exile.' Ovid is thinking of his own exile at Tomi, and declares any one lucky who should be sent to Latium on any terms.

4. **Ausoniis]** 'Latin.' The *Ausŏnes* or *Aurunci* were the inhabitants of the south-western corner of Latium. Hence, in poetry, the name *Ausonia* is given to all Latium and sometimes to all Italy.

Arcade] 'than the Arcadian Evander.'

5. **boves Erytheidas]** 'the cows of Erytheia,' i.e. the cows belonging to Geryones, king of Erytheia, a monster with three bodies. Erytheia itself is the name given by the ancients to a fabulous island somewhere in the far west. First it was supposed to be on the coast of Epirus, and then in the *fretum Gaditanum*, i.e. the Straits of Gibraltar.

applicat] 'lands.'

Heros Claviger] ' the club-bearing hero Hercules.'

6. **emensus longi orbis iter]** 'having accomplished a journey of long circuit' (gen. of measure with epithet). Hercules had now travelled through Europe to Africa as far as Mount Atlas, had then crossed to Erytheia, thence to Gibraltar and over the Pyrenees and Alps into Italy.

7. **domus Tegeaea**] i.e. 'the Arcadian house of Evander.'
Tegea was anciently one of the most important towns of
Arcadia.

9. **Tirynthius hospes**] i.e. Hercules, who was said to have
been brought up at Tiryns near Argos.

12. **aversos**] i.e. 'backwards,' lit. turned away from him.
Propertius (5, 9, 12) fills up the picture, *aversos cauda traxit in
antra boves*. **feros**] *feri* is used in poetry as a substantive instead of *ferae*, 'wild beasts.'

13. **Cacus**] a mythical shepherd robber, whose cave is still
shown near the *Porta Trigemina* at Rome, which was near the
north-west corner of the Aventine.

Aventinae silvae] 'of the forest on Mount Aventine.' He
refers to the state of things before Rome was built. The reference
would be as interesting to a Roman as it is to us to hear of the
meadows in the 'little village of Charing,' or of a snipe shot in
Piccadilly.

15. **pro**] 'in proportion to.'

16. **Mulciber**] Vulcan. The word is said to be connected
with *mulceo:* and is an instance of euphemism, i.e. giving a good
name to something or some god who is really a cause of fear.
So the Furies are called *Eumenides* 'friendly;' the πόντος ἄξεινος
'inhospitable sea' is called the εὔξεινος 'hospitable.' Vulcan, or
fire, is called *Mulciber* that he may cherish, not consume, us.

17. **pro**] 'in place of.'

19. **ora**] 'skulls.'

20. Hercules was worshipped in Italy in connection with
the abolition of human sacrifices, which perhaps is here
typified.

21. **servata male**] 'ill kept,' i.e. lost.

22. **furta**] 'the stolen oxen,' lit. 'the thefts.'

24. **impia antra**] 'the cave of the impious Cacus:' *impia*
because of the murders and cannibalism that took place there.

25. **praestruxerat**] 'he had blocked up the entrance:' *prae*,
'in front.'

obice] (*obex, objicio*) 'with a barrier of a huge broken rock,'
i.e. 'with a huge fragment of rock as a barrier.' *Montis* (gen.
of material) is used instead of *saxi* to indicate the great size
of the stone.

26. **iuga**] 'pairs.'

27. **caelum quoque sederat illis**] 'the heaven too had rested on them,' i.e. when he held up the heavens for Atlas, while the latter was fetching the golden apples of the Hesperides.

30. **subsedit**] 'caved in.'

31. **collata dextra**] 'at close quarters,' *cominus*.

32. **rem gerit**] sc. 'fights.'

33. **quis**=*quibus*. **patrias ad artes**] 'to the arts of his father Vulcan,' i.e. to the use of fire.

35. **Typhoea**] the Greek acc. of *Typhoeus*. Typhoeus, a fearful monster with a hundred heads, terrible eyes and voice, father of the Harpies, and the whirlwinds; whom Jupiter slew with a thunderbolt, and buried under Mount Etna, where he vomits out flames.

37. **occupat**] 'springs upon him:' *occupat* conveys the idea of anticipation, i.e. Hercules springs on Cacus before he can ward off the blow.

adducta] 'raised and drawn back so as to bring it down with the more force.' Milton means the same thing when he says:

'Where the rude axe with *heavèd* stroke
Was never heard the nymphs to daunt.'

38. **sedit**] 'came firmly down upon:' **adversi**, 'opposite,' i.e. the blow was full on his face.

40. **plangit**] 'beats,' as he writhes in the agony of the death-struggle.

II

1. **Vestalis**] The Vestal virgins attended on the temple of Vesta and were bound to virginity for their thirty years' service.

2. **patruo**] i.e. Amulius. Ilia was the daughter of Numitor, who had been deprived of his royal power in Alba Longa by his brother Amulius.

3. **is**] Amulius.

4. **ex istis alter**] 'one of these two.'

5. **recusantes**] 'though revolting at.'

7, 8. 'The Albula, which Tiberinus by being drowned in its waters changed to the Tiber.' That is, the earlier name of the Tiber was Albula, which was changed to Tiber because some Tuscan prince named Tibris or Tiberinus was drowned in it. Ovid calls him *Tiberinus;* Virgil (Aen. 8, 330) calls him *Tibris.*

8. **hibernis tumebat**] i.e. there was a flood.

9. **fora**] By the *fora* Ovid means the *forum Romanum*, the *forum Julium*, and the *forum Augustum*, which were all between the Palatine and Quirinal hills. They were open spaces in which business was transacted. The Greeks called such a place an ἀγορά. The *forum Romanum* was the oldest of the three, and had at one end the *Comitium* and *Curia*. The *forum Julium* was so called because it was made by Julius Caesar B.c. 46, the *forum Augustum*, because made by Augustus B.c. 2.

10. **Maxime Circe**] The Circus Maximus was in the valley (the *vallis Mutia*) between the Palatine and Aventine hills. It was a race-course, said to have been originally formed by Tarquinius Priscus and surrounded by scaffolding for the spectators. Julius Caesar had converted this scaffolding into a splendid building.

11, 12. **neque enim procedere possunt longius**] 'for they couldn't go very far,' i.e. because of the flood.

13. **at—at**] 'Well!'

14. **iste**] 'that one,' pointing to Romulus.

15. **nisi fallit imago**] 'unless appearances are deceitful.'

16. **nescio quem Deum**] 'some god or other.'

18. 'He would have brought you aid in an hour of so much danger.' **praecipiti**] *praeceps*, from *prae-caput*, means properly 'head foremost,' 'headlong;' here it is applied to danger which is imminent or swift.

19. 'If their mother (Ilia) had not been in need of his aid.'

si non introduces a negative supposition, *nisi* introduces an exception.

20. **orba**] 'childless.'

22. **desierat**] *desino*. **deposuitque sinu**] 'and he put the babies down from the folds of his dress.'

23. **sentire**] 'that they had reason and knew what was going to happen to them.'

24. **hi**] the two men.

26. **quantum fati**] 'what a mighty destiny!'

28. **sedet**] 'settles on the ground.'

29. **vestigia**] 'some traces of it.' **quaeque vocatur**] 'and what is now called the *ficus Ruminalis* was then called the *ficus Romula.*' This fig tree was said to have been originally on the Palatine, but to have been transplanted to the Comitium miraculously. The Romans were very superstitious about it, and in A.D. 59 great alarm was felt, Tacitus says, because it seemed dead, though it afterwards shot out again. *Ruminalis* is really derived from *rumis*, an old word for an 'udder,' not from *Romula.*

31. **lupa foeta**] 'a she-wolf who had just had cubs.' It has been said that there are authentic instances of something like this having happened, in cases where she-wolves have lost their cubs and seek to ease their udders.

33. **parum est**] 'is not enough.'

34. **sustinuere**] 'had they the heart to?'

35. **blanditur**] 'coaxes' (*blandus*) takes the dative. **alumnis**] 'nurselings' from *alo.*

36. 'And forms their two bodies with her tongue.' This arose from the false idea that an animal licks her young to form their shape, whereas she only does so to clean them. Hence our proverbial expression 'to lick into shape.' **bina** = *duo*. It properly is a distributive meaning 'two apiece.'

37. **satos**] 'born of' with abl. *Satus* is a participle from *sero, sevi* 'to plant.'

III

1. **simulacra**] 'image;' the singular for the plural. *simulacrum* (ἄγαλμα) is the proper word for the figure of a god, *statua* (ἀνδριάς) for that of a man.

3. **pariente ministra**] 'when her priestess brought forth a child.' The priestesses of Vesta, like nuns, were under an obligation not to marry.

4. 'And the frightened flame shrank beneath its embers.' A fire was always kept alight in the temple of Vesta (Ἑστία, the goddess of the hearth), which fire Aeneas was supposed to have brought with the Penates from Troy.

5. **Amulius**] brother of Numitor, who had driven Numitor from the kingdom of Alba Longa.

6. **opes**] 'government.'

9. **lacte ferino**] 'milk of a wild beast,' i.e. the wolf.

10. **picum**] 'a woodpecker,' which was called Martius, or the bird of Mars; and may therefore be supposed to have helped the sons of Mars.

11, 12. **Larentia—Faustule**] Faustulus, the king's shepherd, picked up the children and took them home to his wife Larentia to rear; in honour of whom the festival of the *Larentalia* was held at Rome, mentioned in line 13.

vestras opes] 'the help which you both gave.'

14. **acceptus Geniis**] December is called 'the favourite month of the Genii,' because in it were celebrated the Saturnalia, in which festival each person was supposed to indulge his *Genius*, i.e. the god who from his birth made him his especial care, and who was supposed to be gratified when the man gratified himself. The Saturnalia (the feast of Saturn) were fixed by Augustus for the 17th, 18th, and 19th of December, and in it were kept up many of the customs afterwards adopted when the season became holy for another reason.

15. **senos**]=*sex.* **annos**] accusative of the duration of time.

16. **flavae barba comae**] 'a new beard of yellow down.' *flavae comae*, the genitive of the material.

18. **Iliadae**] 'the sons of Ilia,' i.e. Romulus and Remus. Ilia was another name of Sylvia, as being a descendant of Aeneas.

iura petita dabant] 'acted as arbitrators at their request,' lit. 'gave legal decisions when asked for.' *jura dare* is said of a judge.

20. **in sua rura**] 'into their proper farmsteads.'

21. **pater editus**] 'the disclosure of their father.'

24. **avo**] Numitor.

26. See the next piece, verse 35.

IV

1. **frater Numitoris**] Amulius.

2. **gemino sub duce**] 'under the leadership of the twins,' Romulus and Remus.

4. **ambigitur**] 'there is a dispute which of the two is to be the founder.'

6. **magna fides avium**] 'great confidence is felt in augury.' See on 7, 2.

7. **nemorosi Palati**] The Palatium, or Mons Palatinus, is called woody to remind us of its state before the city was built; as in the first piece, verse 13, Ovid speaks of the 'Aventine wood.'

9. **ordine**] 'in his turn.'

pacto statur] 'they abide by the agreement.' *statur* is impersonal; for *pacto* look out *pango.*

11. The first step in founding a town was to mark out its limits by cutting a furrow with the plough.

12. 'The festival of Pales was near at hand, the work (of building the city) is started on that day.' The *Palilia* were held on the 21st of April (XI Kal. Mai). *Pales* was a pastoral deity. Part of the ceremony at the festival was running through heaps of lighted hay, hence it is called sometimes *fumosa Palilia.*

13—24. **fossa fit ad solidum**] 'a trench is dug down to firm soil.' It is necessary in laying a foundation to rest it upon soil that has not been moved, to prevent 'settling.' In Ovid's time, when sites in the city had probably been mostly built on before, this would need to be especially attended to.

The ceremonies observed are these: the trench is first dug to the needful depth; then some corn is thrown in and some earth from a neighbouring plot as an assertion of the right of the city over the surrounding district and its crops ; the foundation being laid the trench is filled up, and an altar erected upon it and inaugurated with a burnt sacrifice; from this spot the furrow is cut with a plough drawn by a white cow and a white bull in the line the wall is to take; then the founder offers a prayer to Jupiter, Mars and Vesta.

16. 'And the new altar is inaugurated by lighting a fire on it.'· **fungitur** is active; lit. 'performs a lighted fire.' Cp. *fungi dapibus; fungi lacrimis.*

17. **stivam**] The *stiva* is the handle of the plough which the ploughman holds.

20. **Mavors**] an old form (probably Sabine) of *Mars.* Vesta is called *mater*, though unmarried, as the goddess worshipped at Lavinium the mother city of the Latins.

21. **quosque pium, etc.**] This is added lest any god should be omitted who ought to have been named, on the same principle as that on which the Athenians built an altar to 'the unknown god.'

22. **auspicibus vobis**] 'with your favour.' Abl. absol.

23. 'Long be the life, long be the sway of this imperial land.' *Longa* and *dominae terrae* belong to both clauses.

26, 27. Thunder on the left, birds on the right, were good omens.

28. **exiguo tempore**] 'within a short space of time.'

29. **Celer**] In the earliest times of Rome all knights were called *Celeres*, and perhaps this word only meant a knight at first, but has become a proper name in the legend in course of time.

34. **his**] 'such paltry walls as these.'

35. **rutro** (*ruitrum, a ruendo*) 'a spade.' **occupat**] see 1, 37.

38. **devorat**] 'swallows his tears,' i.e. will not let them appear.

39. **servat**] 'maintains.'

40. **sic**] 'with a similar result.'

V

1. **Ardea**] the capital of the Rutuli, twenty-four miles south of Rome.

2. **lentas obsidione moras**] 'a lingering siege;' lit. 'slow delays in, or, by a siege.' *obsidione* is abl. of instrument.

3. **dum vacat**] 'while there is a lull in the operations:' used here as an impersonal verb.

6. **accipit**] 'entertains.'

rege creatus] 'the king's son,' i.e. Sextus. *Rege* the ablative of origin.

8. **ad patrios Deos**] i.e. 'home.'

9. **torus socialis**] 'our wives.' **ecquid**] merely asks the question.

10. **mutua cura**] i.e. are they thinking of us as we of them ?

13. 'Up gets he to whom Collatia had given a name,' i. e.
L. Tarquinius Collatinus, a great-nephew of Tarquinius Priscus,
and named from Collatia, a town in Latium, of which his father
Egerius was governor.

14, 15. The story is told also in the first book of Livy,
where this speech stands thus: *quin conscendimus equos, invisi-*
musque praesentes nostrarum ingenia? id cuique spectatissimum
sit, quod nec opinato viri adventu occurrerit oculis.

18. in fore] 'at the wicket.' *Foris* is generally used only
in the plural *fores*, the swinging doors in a gateway.

19. fusis per colla coronis] 'with garlands hanging from
her hair down upon her shoulders.' Both men and women
wore flowers in their hair at banquets. But in earlier times it
was thought wrong for a matron to be present where wine was
drunk: as also among the Greeks. So Pentheus in the Bac-
chae of Euripides says:

'For I hold
That where the wine-cup stands upon the board
No woman may be present and be pure.'

20. posito pervigilare mero] 'spending the whole long
night with wine upon the board.' As the Romans dined between two and three in the afternoon, drinking late at night
would be a very conspicuous act of excess even in men.

pervigilare] The *per* has an intensive force.

23—26. Lucretia is discovered preparing wool with which
afterwards to weave a wrapper for her husband.

23. 'By a small lamp her handmaidens were spinning
their tasks of yarn.'

The 'small lamp' is to contrast with the brilliant banquet
of the wife of Sextus. **trahebant]** i. e. were drawing the yarn
from the distaff (*colus*) and twisting it into wool by means of
the spindle (*fusus*). **pensa** are the amounts of yarn weighed
out to each woman to work (*penděre*).

26. lacerna] Ovid uses this word, common in his day, as a
general term for any 'overcoat' or 'wrapper,' although it was
really a dress not known until towards the end of the Republic. It was a fashion borrowed from Gaul.

28. esse super] =*superesse*, 'to be left.'

29. melioribus] 'men better than yourself.' **restas** =
resistis.

32. **stricto ense**] 'when he has once drawn his sword.'

34. **me subit**] 'occurs to me.'

35. **desinit in lacrimas**] 'she finished by bursting into tears.' *in* takes the accus. because *desinere* implies motion, though motion arrested at a point: so, *desinit in piscem mulier formosa superne.* It is an elegant construction to be observed and imitated.

intentι **fil̃a**] the threads which she was holding tight as she drew them off the *colus*.

VI

3. **patrem**] Spurius Lucretius Tricipitinus, who with Brutus was elected first to the consulship on the expulsion of the Tarquins B.C. 509.

5. **habitum**] 'the disorder of her dress and general appearance.'

6. **exequias**] 'funeral rites' (*e- sequor*), **icta** from *ico*. It is rare that any part of the verb is used except *ictus*.

7. **pudibunda**] (*pudere*) 'bashful,' like *moribundus, furibundus, tremebundus*, is an adjective denoting an habitual state and was originally a gerundive.

8. **perennis aquae**] 'a spring.' *perennis* = 'lasting the whole year' (*annus*) and then 'perpetual.'

9. **hinc—hinc**] 'on one side,' 'on the other.'

orant, indicet] *ut* omitted.

10. **caeco metu**] 'with fear of they knew not what.'

12. **ideo**] 'any the more for that,' i.e. though she was at last able to speak she could not even then raise her eyes.

13. **hoc quoque...debebimus?**] lit. 'Shall we owe this too to the Tarquins?' i.e. that I am obliged to tell my own dishonour. In addition to all my other wrongs am I to owe them the shame of this story?

15. **restabant ultima**] 'the worst remained untold.'

17. **facto coactae**] 'the deed of one who had been forced.'

21. **honeste**] 'decently.'

23. **communia damna**] 'a loss that affected them both,' one as father, the other as husband.

24. **decoris**] 'rank.'

25. **fallit**] 'falsifies.' **sua nomina**] plur. for sing., as also *tela* in next line. Ovid has before called Brutus *stulti sapiens imitator*. He is said to have feigned madness to escape the jealousy of the Tarquins.

29. **per tibi ego hunc**] Obs. the order of the words. In solemn oaths the emphatic pronoun is generally put between the *per* and that which it governs. No doubt the old formulas began in that way.

31. **poenas daturum**] 'shall be punished.'

profuga] 'exiled,' cf. 18, 32.

32. **virtus**] 'my valour.'

35. **animi virilis**] genitive of quality.

36. 'And is followed to the tomb by the tears and indignation of the people.'

37. **vulnus inane patet**] 'the gaping wound is before their eyes.' *inane* seems to refer to the appearance of a wound when blood has ceased to flow. Cp. Shakespeare:

' Show you sweet Caesar's wounds, *poor poor dumb mouths*,
And bid them speak for me; but were I Brutus
And Brutus Antony, there were an Antony
Would ruffle up your spirits, *and put a tongue
In every wound* of Caesar that should move
The stones of Rome to rise and mutiny.'

38. **regis facta nefanda**] Not only the crime of Sextus, but the cruelties of Superbus. Livy says *addita superbia ipsius regis, miseriaeque labores plebis in fossas cloacasque exhauriendas demersae*.

39. **fugit**] 'is driven into exile.' The 23rd of February (VII Kal. Mart.) was kept by the Romans in memory of this expulsion of the Tarquins, and the festival was called the *regifugium*.

40. **regnis**] 'to kingly power.'

VII

The quarrel at this time was not so exclusively between Plebeian and Patrician, as between rich and poor, on the subject of the cruel laws of debt, which surrendered the person of a debtor who could not pay entirely into the hands of his creditor.

2. vera fide] 'truth.' *Fides* may be (1) the honour which makes one tell truth, (2) faith, the feeling of belief in the truth of another, (3) credit, i.e. the belief others have in our truth, (4) the trustworthiness or truth of a statement, as here. **dissidet** 'is far from.'

3. Tribunis] The *Tribuni plebis*, whose chief duty it was to watch the interests of the *plebs*, were first appointed in the next year, 493 B.C.

4. in vertice abit] (*abit=abiit*) means 'departed from Rome and was on the top of the Mons Sacer.'
The Mons Sacer was on the right bank of the river Anio, about three miles from Rome.

6. ceres] 'corn.'

7. Bovillis] 'at Bovillae:' locative case. Bovillae was ten miles from Rome on the Via Appia.

8. mundae sedulitatis] (gen. of quality, cf. 6, 35) 'a neat and industrious old woman.' *sedulus* (whence *sedulitas*) is probably from the root *sed-* seen in *sĕd-eo*, *sēd-es*, and means 'industrious,' from the notion of sitting persistently at work.

9. mitra] 'snood,' a scarf wound round the head and then tied under the chin. It was a Greek fashion, and in Italy chiefly used by old women.

redimita capillos] 'bound as to her hair,' the accusative of respect, or Greek accusative as it is sometimes called.

10. fingebat] 'used to shape,' cf. 2, 36.

11. ita] 'just as they were,' i.e. without taking anything to eat with them.

13. pace facta] i.e. a reconciliation between the plebeians and patricians having been made.

signum] 'statue.'

Perennae] i.e. to *Anna Perenna*. The whole story is a later legend to account for the worship of Anna Perenna, which really means the full moon, *Anna* being a feminine of *annus*, and *perenna* an archaism for *perennis*. *Annus* properly means a circle, and *perennis* is from *per-annus*. The title, thus referring to the Moon's revolutions, in this legend is applied to the perpetual (*perennis*) supply of food given by Anna.

---

14. defectis] In ver. 5 *deficio* was constructed as a transitive verb governing the accusative, it is therefore able to admit a past participle passive *defectus*, 'failed by,' i.e. 'in want of something.' So we use 'fail' as an intransitive and transitive verb. We say 'he failed in his effort,' where it is intransitive; and 'you failed me,' where it is transitive.

VIII

1. haec fuit illa dies] i.e. the Ides or 13th of February. Livy says that the Fabii were destroyed on the 18th of July. But Ovid reckons the black day to be that on which they left Rome.

Veientibus arvis] *Vei*, the modern *Isola Farnese*, was an Etruscan city on the river Cremĕra, about 12 miles from Rome. Its territory at this time extended probably up, or nearly so, to the right bank of the Tiber.

3. domus] 'family.' By 'one family undertaking the burden and forces of the city,' Ovid means that the Fabii had determined to bear alone the brunt of the war with the Veientines. They were led out by Kaeso Fabius in his third Consulship, B.C. 479. A main reason for their thus leaving the city seems to have been the dangerous position of Kaeso, who though a patrician had taken part with the plebs.

4. gentiles] 'all of one gens.' **professa]** 'volunteered,' because the offer to carry on the Veientine war was freely made to the Senate: **professus**, *participle passive* of deponent verb *profiteor*.

7. 'There is a passage through the *Porta Carmentalis* nearest to the temple of Janus on the right.' The gate was called the 'Gate of Carmentis' from an altar to *Carmentis* supposed to be the mother of Evander. It had two archways; Ovid says that the road leading through the right-hand one nearest to the temple of Janus is to be avoided as unlucky. The gate was somewhere between the Mons Capitolinus and the river.

9. rapacem] 'rapid,' because of the season, as he explains next line. For ordinarily the Cremera is a small insignificant stream.

12. Tyrrhenum] 'Tuscan.'

13. Libyca] 'African.'

18. **arma caeca**] 'an ambuscade.'

19. **ultima**] 'the extremities.'

21. **rara**] 'scattered at wide intervals.'

22. **virgultis**] 'by brushwood.' The object of leaving a few cattle and men in the plain was first to make the Fabii believe that no one else was near, secondly, to make them scatter in pursuit of the booty.

24. **repente**] 'in a sudden thaw.'

27. **discursibus**] 'raids,' *discurrere* means 'to separate and run in different directions,' as soldiers would when scattering for plunder.

29. **male creditur**] 'ill is it to trust your foe.'

35. 'Like a boar that has been run down far from his covert in the Laurentine forest.' *Laurentum*, on the coast south of the mouth of the Tiber. The *laurus*, 'bay,' grows there in abundance still, and wild-boars are also still plentiful.

39, 40. This merely means that the Fabii were all killed in one day. They had been carrying on the war from their camp on the Cremera for more than a year. Ovid, not caring about historical fact so much as a picturesque story, leaves one in doubt whether he means to imply or not that the Fabii were killed on the same day as that on which they left Rome.

41. **Herculeae**] The Fabii claimed to have descended from Hercules by a daughter of Evander.

45. **olim**] 'hereafter.' **Maxime**] i.e. Quintus Fabius Maximus, called Cunctator from his policy of delaying by which he wore out Hannibal. He was appointed Dictator after the battle of Trasimene, B.C. 217. Ovid is referring to a famous line of Ennius,

unus homo nobis cunctando restituit rem.

IX

1—4. The *Vestalia* or feast of Vesta was on the 9th of June. Part of the ceremony was a procession of matrons with bare feet. This custom Ovid says he had had accounted for by a tradition of a marsh once existing in the Velabrum and spreading into the Forum.

2. **Nova via**] A street branching off from the *via sacra* and running behind the Temple of Vesta into the Velabrum, i.e.

the low ground between 'the north point of the Aventine, the
south point of the Capitoline, and the west point of Palatine
and the river.' It was on the hill, but had apparently been
connected with the forum, either by steps or an inclined path-
way.

4. **sustinui**] 'stopped,'

5. **sensit**] 'perceived my surprise.'

vicina loci] 'who lived near the spot.'

7. **fora**] i.e. the Forum Romanum and the Forum Boarium.

8. 'And a ditch was brimming full with the flood-water of
the river;' or, 'Like a ditch (the ground) was wet with the
flood-water of the river.'

11. **Velabra**] plur. for sing. The road from the Forum to
the Circus Maximus passed through the Velabrum, which is
therefore said 'to usher on the processions.'

12. **cassa**] (connected with *careo*) 'empty,' 'barren.'

13, 14. 'Some diner-out being ferried over the suburban
pool,' i.e. the pools formed by the flooding of the Tiber.

14. **cantat...iacit**] historic presents. 'Used to sing,'...'used
to ejaculate.'

15, 16. Sc. Vertumnus. A statue of this god stood between
the Forum Romanum and Forum Boarium. Ovid supposes the
name to be derived from *vertere* and *amnis*. Its true deriva-
tion is from the participle form in *-umnus*, representing the
Greek *-ὁμενος*. Cf. *Auctumnus* (*augeo*), *alumnus* (*alo*). He is
the god of change, and therefore is said 'to suit himself to
various shapes.'

17. **hic quoque**] i.e. where the *Nova Via* enters the *Forum
Romanum*.

18. **pede velato**] i.e. with shoes on.

19. **stagna**] 'floods.'

X

1. **Vesta**] i.e. the temple of Vesta.

3. **sancti ignes**] See on 3, 4.

5. **ministrae**] i.e. the Vestal virgins.

8. **Metellus**] Lucius Caecilius Metellus, who was Pontifex Maximus. It was said that he lost his eyesight in the performance of this feat, for which he was ever afterwards allowed the privilege of riding to the Senate-house in a carriage. Plutarch says that he recovered his sight after duly propitiating the goddess.

9. **pignora fatalia**] i.e. the Palladium, on the keeping of which the safety of Rome was supposed to depend.

10. **voto**] 'by prayer.'

13. **haurit aquas**] i.e. he takes some water to purify himself before entering the shrine.

tollens manus] The attitude of prayer among the Romans was to stand with the hands raised, the palms being turned to the front and bent backwards; hence *supinae manus*.

14. **sacra**] ' oh, ye holy mysteries !'

No man might enter the temple of Vesta.

16. 'Let Rome be free from evil consequences by my punishment,' i.e. be satisfied with my punishment; let not Rome suffer.

caput = 'person.' *damnum capitis* might mean (1) loss of citizenship, (2) loss of life.

18. **pontificis sui**] 'her own Pontiff.' The Pontifex Maximus had a special connection with the worship of Vesta, one of his principal duties being to appoint the Vestal virgins.

munere] 'by the good offices.'

XI

[You must understand that this is part of a letter which Penelope is supposed to write to her husband Ulysses.]

2. **barbara**] i.e. Trojan. The Greeks called all who did not speak Greek βάρβαροι (*barbari*).

3. **nymphae**] 'brides,' which is an unusual meaning. It nearly always means 'nymphs,' i.e. semi-divine persons.

grata dona] ' thank-offerings.'

4. **illi**] i.e. the returned warriors.

canunt] 'repeat exultingly.'

5. **iusti senes**] The old men are called *justi* because they had the care of legislation and administering justice.

7, 8. They spill a little wine on the table and draw a ground plan of Troy, and the sites of the battles.

7. **posita mensa**] when the second course is put on. The Romans had the courses of their meals brought in ready set out on trays (*mensae*).

8. **Pergama**] properly the citadel of Troy, is here used for Troy itself.

9. **hac**] 'in this direction.' **Simois** is one of the rivers of Troy.

Sigela tellus] The town and promontory of Sigeum, near which in the Trojan war a great part of the fighting took place.

11. **Aeacides**] Achilles, grandson of Aeacus.

tendebat] 'used to pitch his tent.' *Tendere* in this sense is a military term, as you will find in Virgil (Aen. 2, 29), *hic saevus tendebat Achilles*.

12. 'Here mangled Hector frightened the horses into galloping at full speed.'

admissos] lit. 'let go,' as applied to horses, means that they have their head given them, and are at full gallop. This refers to the story of Achilles dragging the body of Hector round the walls of Troy fastened to his chariot.

13, 14. **Nestor**] king of Pylos, whom the son of Ulysses (Telemachus) visited when he went in search of his father.

15. **Rhesum Dolonaque**] Rhesus and Dolon, two heroes killed by Ulysses and Diomede in a night expedition. Rhesus, who was king of Thrace, was killed in his sleep. Dolon met Ulysses and Diomede on his way to reconnoitre the Greek camp, and the two lay in wait for him and killed him.

18. **Thracia castra**] i.e. the camp of Rhesus, king of the Thracians. **tangere**] 'to enter.'

19. **tot**] 'such a number:' they killed thirteen. **uno**] i.e. Diomede.

21. **micuere**] 'palpitated:' *micare* means 'to move quickly,' thence in the sense in which you know it best, 'to glitter' or 'shine.'

22. **Ismariis equis**] i.e. 'the Thracian horses' which Ulysses took from Rhesus. *Ismarus* is a mountain and town in Thrace. **amicum agmen**] i.e. the Greeks.

23. **vestris]** 'of you Greeks.'

24. **solum]** 'level ground.'

26. **dempto fine]** 'for ever,' lit. 'a limit being taken away.'

carendus abest] 'my husband is absent, and I have to submit to his loss.' **carendus]** a passive gerund of *careo*, a verb which governs the ablative, like *utendus* and *fruendus*. The more common construction is the impersonal, *carendum est mihi aliquo*.

27. **aliis—mihi]** 'for others,' 'for me.'

28. **incola victor]** 'the conqueror turned settler.'

29. **seges]** 'cornfield;' sometimes it means the crop itself.

resecandaque falce] 'needing to be cut with the sickle.'

30. 'The soil fattened with Trojan blood overflows with its harvest.' As Byron said of the field of Waterloo, 'How that red rain has made the harvest grow!'

31. 'The ploughshare often strikes against the bones of men who fell in the siege.' So in Southey's ballad of Blenheim Kaspar says of the skulls, 'And often when I go to plough, the ploughshare turns them out.'

34. **in quo orbe]** 'in what part of the world.'

ferreus] 'hard-hearted.'

37. **quam tibi reddat]** 'for him to give you.' The purpose expressed by relative with subjunctive.

XII

[You must remember that this is an extract from a letter which Briseis is supposed to be writing to Achilles.]

1. **reditus]** i.e. a return home to Greece. Achilles had threatened to go home and not fight any more.

2. **sarcina]** 'burden.' It properly means anything 'sewn together' (*sarcio*); then 'a bundle,' 'a load.'

4. **molliat]** 'I have a hand well suited to soften wools,' i.e. to draw them off the distaff (*colus*) skilfully, so that they should be like wool, not thread. This was done by neat manipulation with finger and thumb.

7, 8. Some wife worthy of a father-in-law who is a grand-son of Jove and Aegina, and whom Nereus would not disdain as the wife of his grandson.

The father-in-law is Peleus, son of Jove and Aegina.

The *prosocer* is Nereus, father of Thetis, the mother of Achilles.

9. **data pensa]** See on 5, 23.

10. **minuent colos]** 'shall make the distaffs thinner as I draw them off.'

11. **exagitet]** 'persecute me.' It is a word used in hunt-ing to mean 'drive out of covert.'

12. **aequa]** 'kindly disposed.'

13. **scindi]** 'torn.' **coram]** 'in your presence.'

15. 'Or if it must be so, allow it—so long as I am not left behind by you in contempt.'

. **dum ne]** is used in a negative sentence of this sort, not *dum non:* or sometimes *dummodo ne.*

16. **concutit ossa]** 'makes me tremble to my very bones.'

17. **Agamemnona paenitet]** Agamemnon offered Achilles full reparation, and to give back Briseis if he would come back to the fighting; but Achilles refused.

20. **Hector]** While Achilles sulked in his tent, the Tro-jans continually beat the Greeks, and Hector once nearly suc-ceeded in taking and burning the ships. **opes]** 'forces.'

21. **sed me tamen]** 'but take me back first,' lit. 'me first, however, having been received again.'

22. **preme]** 'chase.'

23. **propter me]** because Agamemnon took me from you.

24. **tristitiae]** 'gloomy temper.'

26—30. **Oenides]** is Meleager, son of Oeneus. There was a war between the Aetolians of Calydon and the Curetes for the skin of the boar killed by Meleager. In this war Meleager killed his mother's brothers. His mother, Althaea, being angry, prayed the gods to slay her son. Then Meleager in his anger at this would not fight any longer for the Aetolians, who were then always beaten by the Curetes. His father, mother and sisters all vainly begged him to go to the fight; but at last he gave way to the prayers of his wife Cleopatra.

28. **devovit**] 'devoted to the infernal gods,' 'cursed.'

31. **felicior illa**] 'she was more fortunate than I am!' Because she could persuade her husband, I cannot.

pro nullo pondere cadunt] 'fall idly, and are of no account.'

XIII

[Oenone is supposed to be writing to Paris.]

1. **tantus**] 'so great a man.'

2. Oenone was said to be the daughter of the river Kebren.

3. **absit reverentia vero**] lit. 'let personal respect be absent from truth,' i.e. 'let no feeling of respect for your rank prevent my speaking the plain truth to you.'

4. **servus**] Paris had been exposed as an infant on Mt Ida, and brought up as a shepherd lad. **tuli**] 'I deigned.'

5. **quis**] 'who but I used to show you?' **saltus**] 'coverts.'

7. **retia**] hunting nets. They used stake nets to surround the covert which they were beating, and into which they drove the animals.

maculis distincta] 'with its wide meshes.'

9, 10. 'You often cut my name on the beeches.' Like the lover in Shakespeare's As You Like It, Act iii. 2, 'There is a man haunts the forest that abuses our young plants with carving Rosalind on their barks.'

12. **crescite**] 'grow on, ye letters, and rise to duly form an inscription that shall tell my tale.' Oenone seems to be thinking of an inscription on a tomb.

titulos] *titulus* is properly the inscription on a statue or the like. **in** indicates the end or object of the action.

14. **hoc carmen**] 'this couplet.'

16. i. e. The whole laws of nature shall be changed.

19. **fatum mihi dixit**] 'told me my fate,' i.e. settled what it was to be.

20. **mutati**] 'changed,' like fine weather to stormy.

22. **venit in arbitrium tuum**] 'came to submit to your decision.' Paris was chosen judge to decide to which of the three goddesses the apple, inscribed 'to the most fair,' should be given.

XIV

[Hypsipyle was queen of Lemnos. Jason visited her there when on the voyage in the Argo. He promised to return to her, but in the interval married Medea. Hypsipyle is here supposed to be writing to him.]

1. **barbara pelex**] 'a foreign mistress.' For *barbara* see on 11, 2.

Argolis, -idos, 'a Greek woman.'

3. **carmina**] 'incantations.'

4. **diraque cantata**] 'and with a sickle over which enchantments have been repeated she cuts magic herbs.'

5, 6. When the Moon or Sun was eclipsed it was imagined that they had been affected by witches.

8. **viva saxa**] 'natural rocks.'

9. **discincta**] 'with her dress ungirded.'

10. **tepidis rogis**] 'funeral pyres still warm,' i.e. when the body had but just been burnt.

11. **devovet**] She devotes to destruction by incantation. Another way was to make a wax figure representing the person whom it was wished to injure, and either to melt it at the fire, or pierce it, as here.

13. **et quae nescierim melius**] 'and things which I am all the better for not knowing.' **male quaeritur**] 'love is ill obtained by magic drugs.'

14. **moribus**] 'character.'

15. **in uno**] i.e. 'in the same.'

17. **scilicet**] 'doubtless.'

tauros] This refers to Medea having helped Jason by her charms to yoke the fire-breathing bulls, when he went for the golden fleece.

te iuga ferre coegit] i.e. the yoke of love.

18. **anguis**] referring to the dragon that guarded the golden fleece.

qua ope] 'the same means by which.'

mulcet] 'bewitches.' θέλγει.

XV

[Ariadne is supposed to be writing to Theseus.]

1, 2. It was early morning, when the hoar frost is on the ground, and birds begin to pipe while still on the boughs. So Tennyson talks of ' the earliest pipe of half-awakened birds.'

3. **a somno languida**] 'languid from sleep.' *a somno* has a sense from the combined notions of ' by sleep' as an instrument, and ' after sleep.'

5. **nullus erat**] ' there was no Theseus.'

The simplicity of these pretty lines is full of pathos. They may again remind us of Tennyson :

> ' Tears of the widower, when he sees
> A late-lost form that sleep reveals,
> And moves his doubtful arms, and feels
> Her place is empty, fall like these.'

9. **adductis**] ' brought violently against it.'

10. **e somno**] ' after sleep.' **ut erat**] ' just as it was.'

21. **animus**] ' excitement.'

22. ' I take in the deep ocean in my survey.'

metior] ' I measure' is used metaphorically much as our word measure is, meaning ' I go over.'

23. **usa sum**] 'I have experienced.'

24. **praecipiti**] ' swift.' See on 2, 18.

carbasa] neut. pl. from *carbasus*, fem. *Carbasus* appears to be a Sanskrit word for ' cotton.'

25. ' I saw—or at least when I thought I saw.'

27. **illo**] sc. *dolore*.

30. **numerum suum**] 'its full freight,' ' the full number of its passengers.'

31. **plangore**] ' by beating my breast' (*plangere*).

32. **verbera cum verbis**] The words are suggested by the similarity of sound, but it can scarcely be called a pun.

34. **iactatae...manus**] ' my hands tossed wildly made signals.'

35. **velamina**] 'a veil.'

36. **scilicet**] belongs to *oblitos*. 'To remind those who as I fondly tried to think had only forgotten me.' *Scilicet* shows that she knows that they had not really forgotten her, but purposely left her.

37. **tum denique**] 'not till then.'

38. **genae**] 'eye-balls.'

XVI

[Laodamia is writing to her husband, Protesilaus.]

1. **sors**] 'an oracle.' The answers of oracles were given in different ways, among others by drawing lots, *sortes*. Hence in poetry *sors* may stand for an oracle generally.

2. **Danaum**] gen. plur.

Troada] *Troas*, fem. adject., formed like *Arcas, Arcados*. In these Greek words the termination -*ă* in the accusative is preserved, as also that of -*ăs* in the plural, see 14, 1 *Argolidas*, and *Thesea* from *Theseus*, 15, 28.

4. **strenuus**] 'over active' or 'bold.' This word is connected with Gr. στρῆνος, 'excess of strength,' and our *strong*.

7. **novissimus**] 'last.'

9. **remoque veloque**] to use oar and sail at the same time would be to make all the haste possible.

13. **simulacra noctis adoro**] 'I pray to ghosts of the night,' i.e. the ghosts that appear in the night. The Greeks and Romans looked upon the Manes or Spirits of the departed as divine and needing to be propitiated, cf. 6, 29.

14. **fumo meo**] i.e. a sacrifice from me.

Thessalis] a fem. adj. from *Thessalus*, like *Argolis* in 14, 1.

15, 16. **qua...mero**] 'with which tear the flame spirts out again as it is wont to do when wine is poured in it.'

This would be a good omen; and she takes pleasure in it until she recalls again the idea of Troy and all the dangers of the expedition.

mero] It was customary to extinguish the dying embers of funeral piles and altars with wine, which would generally make the fire just blaze up and then go out.

19, 20. The Greek ships were long detained at Aulis by contrary winds. ·

invitis aquis] 'in spite of the unfavourable state of the sea.'

21, 22. 'Not one of you would even come home in the teeth of the wind, fancy going away from it in a storm !'

The emphatic words are *in patriam* and *a patria*.

26. **non subiti casus]** genit. **mora** belongs both to *casûs* and *numinis*. 'That delay is not come from mere chance, it comes from God.' *Mora casus...numinis*, 'delay caused by chance...by God,' a subjective genitive. *Subitus* is here not exactly ' sudden,' but more what we mean by 'random.'

28. **Inachiae]** 'Argive,' from Inachus, a primitive king of Argos.

XVII

1, 2. 'That you may know what sort of person I, the well-known sportive poet of soft love, was—take these lines, Posterity.'

[Before his exile Ovid was chiefly known by love poetry. Though his greatest work the Metamorphoses was written and his Fasti partly so, they had not been published.]

3. **Sulmo]** a town of the Peligni, seven miles south of Corfinium and about ninety from Rome. Ovid often speaks of its healthiness and of its well-watered district. It stood in the valley of the *Gizio*, a tributary of the Aternus.

6. **cum...pari]** i.e. B.C. 43, when the two consuls Hirtius and Pansa fell in the battle against Antony at Mutina (Modena).

7. **si quid id est]** 'if it is anything.' Ovid evidently thinks it a considerable thing. **ordinis]** sc. *equestris*. What he means by being 'an heir from many generations of the equestrian order' is that his ancestors had belonged to it for many generations. But in truth all members of the *ordo equester* may be said in a sense to be so *munere fortunae*, because since the Lex Sempronia, B.C. 122, everybody possessed of property of the value of 400,000 sesterces was *ipso facto* an eques. Ovid however makes the very common boast that his family had enjoyed the requisite fortune for many generations.

9. **stirps]** 'scion.'

11. **natalibus]** 'birthdays.'

12. **liba]** 'sacrificial cakes.' On a birthday sacrifice was made to a man's protecting genius, and friends made visits and presents.

13, 14. 'This is, of the five days sacred to armed Minerva, that one which is wont to be first made bloody by fighting,' i.e. the first one on which gladiatorial combats were held.

The *quinquatria* of Minerva began on the 19th of March and lasted five days. The shows of gladiators did not commence till the second day (*sanguine prima vacat*, F. 3, 811); consequently Ovid means that he was born on the 20th of March.

15. **protinus]** 'from the first.'

16. **insignes ab arte]** illustrious for their skill, i.e. in rhetoric. For the *ab*, cf. 15, 3.

Urbis] i.e. Rome.

19. **coelestia sacra]** 'heavenly mysteries,' i.e. of the Muses.

22. **Maeonides]** i.e. Homer, who is often so called, from Maeonia or Lydia being assigned as his native place by some traditions. Professor Ramsay says 'Of the seven cities which claimed this honour—Smyrna, Chios, Colophon, Salamis, Rhodos, Argos, Athenae—two were in Maeonia and one an island on its coast.'

24. **modis]** 'the trammels of metre.'

25. Comp. Pope, 'I lisped in numbers for the numbers came.'

numeros ad aptos] 'to the proper metre.'

28. **liberior toga]** i.e. the *toga virilis*, which boys assumed at ages varying from 15 to 17. Before that they wore the *toga praetexta*. Ovid calls it *liberior*, because after this ceremony a youth was supposed to be at liberty to enter into the active life of the Forum, although he probably did not actually do so until later. He was liable for military service after 17.

29. The purple with a broad stripe is put on our shoulders, i.e. we wore the *laticlavia*. In the time of the republic equites wore the *angusticlavia*, or toga with narrow stripe, and a gold ring, and only Senators wore the *laticlavia*, or toga with broad purple stripe. In Ovid's time, however there were two classes

of equites; the first of which, *equites illustres* or *splendidi*, men possessed of a senatorial fortune, and descended from ancestors who had held senatorial rank, wore the *laticlavia*.

33, 34. 'I obtained the first office possible for one of my tender years.' A man could not hold a Curule office, which gave an entrée to the Senate, until he was 36; but there were several minor offices which he might hold, and which were looked upon as steps to the higher offices. Of these Ovid here says that he held that of *triumvir*, one of a commission of three, several of which, for various purposes, e. g. *triumviri monetales, capitales, etc.*, existed.

35. **curia restabat**] i. e. 'the next step was to obtain a Curule office, and so enter the Senate.' The first Curule office to obtain was that of *Curule Aedile*, which a man might be elected to at 36, according to the *lex annalis* or law to regulate ages.

clavi mensura coacta est] '(but instead of my doing so) my *laticlavia* was changed to the *angusticlavia*,' i. e. I left the ranks of the *illustres equites*, the candidates for higher offices, and retired into the private life of an ordinary eques.

36. **illud onus**] 'that burden,' i. e. of public life and senatorial rank.

39. **Aoniae Sorores**] The Muses are called Aonian from Mount Helicon in Boeotia, a country anciently called Aonia.

40. **iudicio meo**] 'in my real unbiassed judgment.'

41, 42. 'I reverenced every poet as almost divine.'

43—54. The names of the poets, whom Ovid knew or saw in his youth. Of these Propertius (d. B.C. 16), Horatius (d. B.C. 8), Vergilius (d. B.C.19), Tibullus (d. B.C. 18), are too well known to require any notice. The works of the others, Macer, Ponticus, Bassus, Gallus, are lost, and not very much is known about the men.

(1) **Aemilius Macer** died in B.C. 16, the author as here mentioned of a poem on birds, reptiles, and simples.

(2) **Ponticus**, only known as the author of an heroic poem on the Theban war.

(3) **Bassus**, unknown.

(4) **Gallus**. Caius Cornelius Gallus is the most considerable personage of these four. He was born about 66 B.C. at Forum Julii (Fréjus) in Gaul, and died B.C. 26. He was

a contemporary and a school-fellow of Virgil, and his great friend. He was with Octavian at Actium, by whom he was afterwards made Prefect of Egypt. His principal known work was a collection of Elegies in four books. He killed himself because he fell into disgrace and was deprived of his offices and property.

45. **ignes**] 'love poems;' *ignis* is a common word for 'love' in poetry, and here it stands for the description of love.

46. **iure sodalitio**] 'but the ties of fellowship,' i.e. by belonging to the same *sodalitas* or club. We cannot tell whether this *sodalitas* was political or merely social. Probably the latter.

48. **convictus mei**] 'of my set' (*cum...vivere*).

49. **numerosus**] 'skilled in many metres,' referring to the various lyric metres employed by Horace.

50. 'Whilst on his Italian lyre he strikes his notes of cultured song.'

ferit] because the lyre is played by striking the strings with a quill or *plectrum* (πλήσσω).

For **Ausonia** see on 1, 4.

culta] Horace's songs are called *culta*, because written in metres many of them new to Latin poets, and learnt and introduced from Greek poetry.

51. **Vergilium**] Virgil died B.C. 19.

Tibullo] Tibullus probably died in B.C. 18, when Ovid was 25 years old.

53. **successor**] That is, Ovid regards the leading Elegiac poets to have been successively Gallus, Tibullus, Propertius, himself.

56. **Thalia**] was the muse of Comedy. But Ovid uses her name as a general one for the muse of Poetry.

57. **legi**] i.e. 'I recited.' A poet at Rome not being able to have his poems printed and so circulated, began by reading them either publicly or to invited audiences. The references to this custom are very frequent.

62. **emendaturis**] 'sure to correct all faults' (*mendae*).

63. **cum fugerem**] 'when I was going into exile.' Ovid says elsewhere that when he was exiled he had written the Metamorphoses, and that he burnt the book; but that others

had copies (which he probably knew quite well), and so they survived.

64. iratus studio] Ovid is 'angry with his calling and his poems,' because one of them, the 'Art of Love,' was the ostensible cause of his banishment.

67. hoc] 'this sort of person,' i.e. prone to fall in love.

igni] is the ablative. The older form of the ablative of -*i* stems was in *i*, e.g. *turri*. But *ignis* may have both *igne* and *igni* in the ablative.

68. fabula] 'scandal.'

74. sustinuit] 'had the courage to be.'

77, 78. That is, Ovid's father died at the age of 90. The *lustrum* properly meant the sacrifice of purification at the end of every five years offered for the whole people at the time of the taking of the *census*. Then it was used to express a space of five years. Ovid says his father had added nine lustra to nine lustra, i.e. 45+45.

80. iusta] 'funeral rites.'

81. tempestive] 'in good time.'

82. poenae] i.e. my exile.

83. me felicem] like *me miserum*, the accusative in exclamations.

88. 'And if the charges against me are discussed in the forum of Hades.'

Stygio] Styx, 'the river of loathing' (στυγέω), one of the rivers of the infernal regions.

90. errorem] The ostensible cause of Ovid's banishment was the immorality of his Ars Amoris. He always asserts, however, that there was another cause, which was a mistake of his, not a fault. Something had happened which he unfortunately knew and saw. What this was has never been clearly ascertained. But it has been gathered, from his various notices of it, that it was something connected with Julia, the granddaughter of Augustus, who was a woman of abandoned character, and was banished about the same time as Ovid, and some of whose debaucheries Ovid may have connived at or assisted.

91. manibus] 'for the spirits of the departed.'

95, 6. 'And since my birth the winning horse garlanded with Pisaean olive had ten times borne off the prize,' i.e. there had been ten Olympic games, which were held at Olympia in Elis, not far from Pisa.

As Ovid was 51 years old at the time of his banishment there had really been twelve Olympic contests in his life. But he confuses a Greek Olympiad (4 years) with a Latin Lustrum (5 years).

According to the Greek reckoning Ovid was born in the 2nd year of the 184th Olympiad, and was banished in the third year of the 196th.

vinctus oliva...equus] A garland of wild olive was the prize at the Olympic games. The horse is here said to be crowned with it instead of the man.

97. **Tomitas]** the Tomitae, the people of Tomi. The modern name is Tomisvar, or perhaps Kustenji in Bulgaria, about 200 miles north of Constantinople, on the shores of the Black Sea. Tomi was a colony of Miletus.

98. **Principis]** of the Emperor. *Princeps*, which meant originally *Princeps Senatus*, was the title most affected by the Emperors, who in every way tried to keep up the fiction of being the chiefs of a free state, in which the institutions of the Republic were in force.

XVIII

1. **subit]** 'occurs to my mind,' cf. 16, 17; 5, 34.

imago] 'idea,' cf. 5, 33.

4. **nunc quoque]** 'even at this distance of time.' Ovid was a year on his journey to Tomi from Rome.

6. **Ausoniae]** sc. Italy. See on 1, 4.

7. 'I had neither had inclination nor sufficient time to make preparations:' lit. 'fitted to one preparing.'

8. **torpuerant]** 'had grown callous,' and therefore had taken no trouble.

10. **vestis opisve]** *cura* is understood from previous line: 'clothes or money.' *opis* is not often found in singular except in accusative *opem* 'help,' and ablative *ope*.

11, 12. **non aliter...]** 'I was just as one who is struck by lightning, and though alive unconscious.'

13. **dolor ipse]** ' the pang of grief itself.'

15. **extremum]** ' for the last time.'

16. **unus et alter]** ' one *or* two.'

18. **imbre]** 'a shower of tears.'

indignas] ' that did not deserve such sorrow.'

19. 'My daughter was away from Rome in the opposite direction (i.e. to that in which I was going), on the coast of Libya.' We do not know who the husband of Ovid's daughter was, but he probably had some provincial office in Africa.

20. **certior esse]** ' to be informed.'

22. **intus]** ' indoors.' **funeris]** ' funeral.'

23. **femina, virque]** sing. for plur., 'women and men alike.'

25. **in parvo]** 'in a matter on a small scale.'

26. Troy naturally suggests itself to Ovid as a model of disaster and dismay as it did to Shakespeare :

'Even such a man, so faint, so spiritless,
So dull, so dead in look, so woebegone,
Drew Priam's curtains in the dead of night,
And would have told him half his Troy was burnt.'

cum caperetur] ' when it was being taken.'

32. **accedam]** 'I shall be added.' Translate : 'I shall be but a small additional weight to the vessel of your exile.' The vessel is called *profuga* because carrying a banished man. Cf. 6. 31.

sarcina] Cf. 12. 2.

34. **pietas]** ' dutiful affection.'

35. **sic]** ' to the same effect.'

36. **dedit manus]** ' gave in.' *dare manus* came to mean ' to be conquered,' from the habit of holding up the hands as a sign of giving up in a fight.

utilitate] The 'expediency' Ovid refers to was probably connected with the safe keeping of his property, which as his punishment was not *exilium* but *relegatio* still remained his own, but would doubtless suffer if there was no one in Rome he could trust to look to his interests.

37. **illud]** i.e. *egredi*, 'if *going* it can be called and not rather a being borne out in funeral procession.'

38. **squalidus]** ' clad in mourning.'

immissis] 'with hair falling over unshorn cheeks.' The Romans of Ovid's time either wore no hair on their faces or exceedingly neatly trimmed beards; so one rule for a dandy Ovid gives is *sit coma sit doctâ barba resecta manu.* A neglect of this was a sign of mourning.

39. illa] my wife. tenebris obortis] 'with a sudden darkness upon her eyes,' i.e. fainting. For *obortis* cf. *lacrymas obortas,* 4, 137.

41. ut] 'when.' resurrexit and membra levavit are not merely repetitions: *membra levare* implies difficulty and previous faintness.

43. se modo] sc. *desertam.*

45. nataeve meumve corpus] 'the body of her daughter or of me.'

47. ponere sensus] 'to get rid of sensation.'

49. quoniam sic fata tulerunt] 'since the fates have so ordered it,' i.e. that I should be absent from her. *tulerunt* is used as though an intransitive in these phrases. Cf. *ita fert voluntas,* 'that is my desire.'

XIX

1—4. Cp. Ps. 107, 26, 'They are carried up to the heaven, and down again to the deep; their soul melteth away because of their trouble.'

3. diducto aequore] 'as the sea yawns.'

6. hic...ille] 'the former,'...'the latter.'

7. 'The wave of the sea knows not which master to obey,' i.e. which of the four winds.

9. purpureo ab ortu] 'from the purple east.'

10. sero vespere missus] 'starting from the west,' lit. from the late evening. That is, where the sun is in the late evening.

11. bacchatur] lit. 'plays the Bacchant.' The Bacchanalian women were inspired with madness by Bacchus. *Bacchari* therefore means to 'revel madly.'

Arcto] the North Pole. Properly, the Bear, or Constellation of the Great Bear.

12. **adversa fronte**] 'front to front,' i.e. in opposite directions, and so meeting each other.

14. **ars**] i.e. the art of navigation.

19. **at...**] 'however it is some consolation that my wife knows nothing of all this, my exile is all that grieves her.'

20. **hoc nostri mali**] 'thus much of my misfortune and no more.' Cf. 20. 5. A partitive gen.

23. **o bene**] understand *factum est*, 'ah how lucky it was that, &c.' **conscendere**] sc. *navem*, 'embark.' **passus** for *passus sum*.

25. **ut peream**] 'even though I perish.' Cp. 22, 20.

26. 'I shall survive at least in half of myself.' **dimidia parte**, abl. of part affected.

28. **aetherio axe**] 'the welkin.' *Axis*, the axle, on which the sky was supposed to revolve, came to be used for the sky itself. **fragor**] 'crash,' from root of *frango*.

29. **laterum tabulae**] 'the timbers of the ship's sides.'

30. **balistae**] (βάλλειν) 'stone-throwing machines.' These machines were used to throw huge stones against walls; and a smaller sort were used like field-cannon, being transported from place to place on carts.

31, 32. 'Every tenth wave is the biggest.'

33. **genus leti**] 'the sort of death.'

35, 36. **est aliquid...**] ''tis something to be buried on dry land, if one must die.'

fato suo] 'at one's appointed time.'

38. **aliqua sepulcra**] 'some burial.' The plural sepulcra seems here to be used for funeral ceremony.

XX

[Ovid is writing to his wife from Tomi.]

2. **aeger eram**] 'I was sick,' i.e. when I was writing this. The imperfect is the usual tense employed in letters; the writer puts himself in the place of the receiver of the letter.

5. **quid animi...putes**] what would you think my feelings were? *quid animi*, 'what of mind?' Cf. 19, 20.

6. **Sauromatas Getasque**] 'between the Sauromatae and Getae.' The *Getae* were the inhabitants of Dacia, which was not subdued by the Romans until A.D. 101. The *Sauromatae* were a tribe near the southern shores of the Maeotis Palus (Sea of Azof).

10. **Apollinea arte**] i.e. the art of medicine. Apollo was the god of medicine as well as song, and was father of Aesculapius.

12. **narrando**] 'by telling stories.'

14. **subit**] 'occurs to my mind,' see 5, 34 and index.

15. **vincis**] 'you are of more importance.'

16. **plus parte**] 'more than half.'

19, 20. **quin etiam sic...ut...**] 'Nay more, they say that I never wandered in my speech without your name being on my lips in my delirium.'

loqui aliena, 'to speak beside the purpose,' i.e. deliriously.

sic...ut] Lit. 'only in such way that your name was, etc.' They may be translated by 'though' and 'yet.' Cf. Cic. *ita eras lupercus ut consul esse meminisse deberes*, 'though you were a lupercus yet you should have remembered that you were a consul.'

21. 'Even if I were dying, and my tongue were cleaving to the roof of my mouth.'

23. 'Suppose some servant were to announce that his mistress had come.'

dominam] 'my wife.'

24. **vigoris**] 'of recovered strength.'

XXI

[The excessive hardness of the winter at Tomi here described by Ovid is unlike what we know of its climate. However, it is said that the cold in Bulgaria is at times much greater than would be expected from its latitude; and Ovid may have experienced an unusually hard winter, and at the same time be willing to paint everything in the worst possible colours. He gives precise details which certainly have the appearance of personal experience : especially he notices the fact mentioned in 49, 50, of fishes retaining their vitality when embedded in ice, which Mr Church points out Ovid was not likely to know except from personal observation. It is somewhat remarkable that Virgil, who could only know by report, describes this neighbourhood in much the same language. Georg. 3, 349—383.

3. **prior, altera]** 'the snow of the previous year,' 'a second fall.'

4. **bima]** 'two years old.'

5. **commoti]** 'when it has begun to blow a storm,' lit. 'has been set in motion.'

7. **pellibus et sutis braccis]** 'with skins and sewn trowsers,' means ' with trousers of sewn skins :' like *maculis distinctus et auro*, which is the same as *maculis aureis distinctus*. The trowsers here meant are what are called *braccae laxae* (θύλακοι) 'loose trowsers,' not breeches fitting close. Elsewhere Ovid says *Pellibus et laxis arcent mala frigora braccis*. Look out *braccae* in Dict. of Antiquities.

11. **nuda...vina]** By the 'wine standing naked' Ovid means that it will stand without the covering of the jar, from which it can be taken out in a frozen mass and set up on end.

12. **nec hausta meri sed data frusta]** 'and they swallow not portions of wine drawn out, but bits handed to them.' Grammatically *frusta* belongs both to *hausta* and *data*, but for the sense some such word as *pocula* must be understood with *hausta*. Cf. Virgil, G. 3,

> *caeduntque securibus humida vina.*

13. **concrescant]** 'are frozen over.'

14. **fragiles aquae]** 'water that can be broken' (instead of poured), i.e. ice.

15. **papyrifero amne]** i.e. the Nile. The *papyrus* no longer exists in the Nile.

17, 18. **Hister]** The Danube is never now frozen over at its mouth, though higher up stream it is. **tectis aquis]** 'with its waters covered in by ice.' **caeruleos latices]** 'its blue waters.' The colour of the Danube is well known.

21. **perque novos pontes]** 'and over novel bridges,' i.e. of ice.

22. **Sarmatici]** Sarmatia and Sarmaticus are used in a general sense to include all the tribes on the north shore of the Black Sea.

24. **ratam debet**] 'a witness ought to have firm credit:' for *fides* see on 7, 2. The only 'interest' Ovid can have had in exaggerating these details is to move compassion for himself in Augustus, and secure his recall or at least a change in his place of exile.

25. **pontum**] i.e. the Black Sea. The harbour of Odessa and others in the Black Sea are blocked in winter now, but not those in the neighbourhood of Tomi.

26. **lubrica testa**] 'a slippery shell,' a coating of ice.

27. **durum calcavimus aequor**] 'I have trodden on the sea which was all hard beneath my feet.'

29, 30. **Leandre**] Leander was drowned while swimming across the Hellespont to Abydos to visit Hero. Mr Church gives the following version of this couplet:

'Had such, Leander, been the sea
　　That flowed betwixt thy love and thee,
Never on Helles' narrow strait
　　Had come the scandal of thy fate.'

30. **angustae crimen aquae**] 'a charge against the narrow strait,' i.e. of having drowned Leander. So in 1, 13 Cacus is called *Aventinae infamia sylvae*.

31. **pandi delphines**] 'curly dolphins.' For *pandi*, cf. *pandus asellus*.

34. **obsesso gurgite**] 'on the flood hemmed in with ice.'

37, 8. **pisces haerere ligatos**] 'fish imprisoned in ice.' It is true that fish thus embedded will long retain life.

40. **redundatas flumine aquas**] 'the waters which over-flowed from the river,' see 9, 8.

cogit] ' freezes.'

41. **aequato**] 'made a level surface of ice.'

42. **invehitur**] 'rides down upon us.' *invehi* is middle, and has a participle *invehens*.

47. **stridentia**] 'creaking.'

51. **hamatis**] 'barbed.' Ovid elsewhere has *arundo hamata*. Anything crooked may be called a *hamus*, among other things the *barbs* of an arrowhead.

52. **tinctile**] 'smeared on them,' or 'in which they are dipped' (*tingere*).

54. **hostica**] lit. 'by the invader.'

XXII

1. **finitimis armis**] ‘the wars of the neighbouring tribes.’ Cf. 20, 6.

3. **quod**] sc. *carmen.*

5. **obsto**] stand up against.

6. **taedia**] ‘disgust,’ i.e. that I do not commit suicide.

7, 8. **gratia**] ‘Thanks to you, my Muse!’ Ovid means that the writing of poetry has been his one consolation and employment; it has kept him from suicide, made him forget Tomi, and given him the enjoyment of fame in his lifetime. So Coleridge says, ‘Poetry has been to me its own exceeding great reward: it has soothed my afflictions; it has multiplied and refined my enjoyments, it has endeared solitude.’

10. **in medio Helicone**] ‘on mid Helicon,’ i.e. on the Mount of the Muses. See on 17, 39.

By the Muses taking him from the Danube and placing him on mid Helicon, Ovid means that in his poetical pursuits he forgets the dreary neighbourhood of the Danube.

11. **vivo**] ‘while still alive.’

13. **detrectat**] ‘detracts from.’   **iniquo**] ‘hostile.’

14. **de nostris**] sc. *operibus.*

18. **plurimus legor**] ‘I am read by a very great number of people,’ or perhaps ‘the greatest number of any poet.’ As a man might boast now-a-days of having the largest circulation.

20. **ut**] ‘though.’

21, 22. **favore...iure**] ‘by partiality,’...‘deservedly,’ ablatives of manner.

carmine] ‘by means of my poetry,’ the ablative of the effective cause.

grates ago] ‘I thank.’   *Grates* is only plural and is seldom found except in nom. and accus.

INDEX.

CAMBRIDGE: PRINTED BY C. J. CLAY, M.A., AT THE UNIVERSITY PRESS.

www.ingramcontent.com/pod-product-compliance
Lightning Source LLC
Chambersburg PA
CBHW020305090426
42735CB00009B/1229